THE
END
of
BOYS

THE
END
of
BOYS

PETER BROWN
HOFFMEISTER

Soft Skull Press
AN IMPRINT OF COUNTERPOINT

Note: This book is a work of nonfiction, and I have attempted to render the story accurately. Using journal entries, transcripts, letters, and conversations with friends, my parents, and siblings, I have supplemented my own memory of the events. But there will be imperfections, and for those I apologize. Also, some names of people and places have been changed to protect the innocent and the guilty.

Library of Congress Cataloging-in-Publication Data

Hoffmeister, Peter Brown.
  The end of boys / Peter Brown Hoffmeister.
    p. cm.
  ISBN 978-1-59376-420-3 (pbk.)
  1. Hoffmeister, Peter Brown. 2. Teenage boys—Biography. 3. Problem children—Biography. 4. Obsessive-compulsive disorder. I. Title.
  HQ797.H57 2011
  155.45'3092—dc22
  [B]
                                    2011005461
Printed in the United States of America

Soft Skull Press
An imprint of Counterpoint
1919 Fifth Street
Berkeley, CA 94710

www.softskull.com

Distributed by Publishers Group West

10 9 8 7 6 5 4 3 2 1

For Cooper

(who ate the evidence)

| CONTENTS |

⊞

The Cat

I sneak the shotgun. Load the three yellow cartridges printed with "Remington 20 Gauge." Snap the action shut. Aim at items in my room: the lamp, my baseball card collection, a picture of my parents. Finger the trigger.

I am alone. Fourteen.

I ease the stock down from my shoulder and turn the gun back toward myself. Stare down the barrel. Tap my index finger against the hollow, producing a sucking sound. I put my mouth over the barrel. Taste the metal, feel the air inside, the barrel's breath on my tongue. I relax my lips and close my eyes. I can smell the invisible beginnings of rust.

The voice is not there. But the hum is. It slides pitches higher, a rush of warm air, the electric collision of a storm front. I nod my head, taking the loaded gun with me. Up and down. I put my hands around the single barrel, closing my fingers, steadying the steel in my mouth, against my teeth, lips sliding on gun oil.

Sitting on the edge of the bed, eight years old, in the middle of the night. Awake. Watching the wall. The wall a machine. Ball bearings clink. Slide through chutes. Drop. The language of working metal. Rhythm in front of me, in front of my open eyes. A wall alive. I have a fantasy that a big dog attacks me. A Rottweiler. Its neck muscles are rolled telephone cables under the loose sweatshirt of its skin. Maybe I'll go to art school and become a painter like my mother.

I open my eyes. Ease the gun out. The sight catches on my two front teeth and clicks. The hum exhales. I can feel the release of nervous animal sweat, the drip underneath my arms.

My father is coming home from work, from the hospital. He'll check my math and science work. I unload the gun and sneak it back down. My mother is feeding applesauce to my baby brother, Ellis, in the kitchen. She doesn't see me.

Before I shelve the gun in the basement, I hold it one more time. Loaded shotgun and no mirrors. It doesn't matter that I am a fourteen-year-old homeschooled boy and five feet two inches tall, that I've never kissed a girl. It doesn't matter that I obey the voice.

By eighth grade, homeschool means that I teach myself. When I was younger, my mother spent hours each day teaching the four of us children what she called "cultural literacy" on beautiful twelve-by-twelve flashcards: the states; Central American countries, capitals, and chief exports; great works of European art; the world's inventors; birds of the United States; the bugs of the Southwest; French verbs and nouns. She named our school Hoffmeister Country Day, HCD, and we were required to wear uniforms. Sometimes. The rules always changed. But that was grade school. Now my mother doesn't teach me anything, and I don't have to dress any particular way. Other than my father checking my math and science homework, I manage my own education.

That spring, there was the cat. The alley cat. Orange and dirty as a public restroom, an abscess seeping around its collar. Its hair was darker behind its neck, wet with pus, clumped. Other than scaring him off our porch so he wouldn't steal our own cat's food, I never thought much of him.

My baby brother, Ellis, nine months old, looked as if his mouth were squirreling marshmallows, puffed cheeks and Michelangelo-cherub lips. He had fallen asleep in his car seat on the way home from the store, and my mother had pulled his seat out to let him keep resting in the shade of the garden while she weeded and spoke softly to her plants. My mother rubbed her fingers over the tops of her English Breakfast, saying, "Well, aren't you strong little guys. Yes, you are. Yes, you are." This was nothing new. I'd caught her reading Evelyn Waugh novels to her flowers.

She continued whispering and weeding as the alley cat crept up, climbed, and sat on Ellis's chest. Ellis woke to the cat on his face, to the smell of the wet abscess seep. He shrieked. And the cat reacted, slashed out. One claw caught under Ellis's right eye. The cut opened across his cheek, and he shrieked again, louder.

My mother lunged, but the cat got away through the boxwoods.

Because I manage my own school schedule, I've moved my math and science classes to later in the day, reading *Lord of the Rings* for three hours instead, curled in a living room wingback.

My mother lurches through the front door, yelling and swearing. She's holding Ellis against her shoulder as though he's a day old, cradling him as if his head might fall off.

Ellis cries in short little jerks.

"What happened?"

She says, "Shit shit shit shit . . . "

I follow her as she runs into the kitchen.

She wets a paper towel and lowers Ellis to the counter. I see the cut on his cheek, not deep, but long and dark and bleeding steadily. My mother dabs at his cheek with the wet paper towel, thinning the blood as she thins her oils with turpentine. Dark red comes up through the watery pink.

"What happened?"

My mother presses on the cut. "It was a cat."

"What? What cat?"

"It was that mangy orange cat." My mother hardly moves her lips. She looks as if she's spitting coffee grounds between her teeth.

"What mangy orange cat?"

She brushes Ellis's cheek hard with the folded paper towel, brushes again, then holds it down. His cheek goes white from the pressure. My mother growls, "I've got to get this cut clean. Disgusting . . . " She looks at me. "It was that orange alley cat that's always getting into fights on our back porch."

"Oh. The one with the neck rot?"

"Yes. *That* cat scratched my baby's face."

Ellis is crying still, but he's also looking at us now with his huge blue eyes. His pain is changing to curiosity.

My mother doesn't notice. She cradles Ellis back against her shoulder, rubs and pats his back. She looks at me. "Your father's at work. He can't help us with this. So you're the man of the house now."

I nod. "Okay."

"And I need you to take care of that cat."

I nod again, "Okay," but I don't know what she means. We don't have cat traps hanging from sixteen-penny nails around the house.

My mother directs me once more, this time with her index finger tapping my chest. "You're the man of the house now, Peter. So take care of it."

My mind goes through a series of questions. "Are you telling me to kill it?" The possibility of actually shooting the shotgun excites me.

My mother has already turned away, heading toward the base of the stairs. She says, without looking back, "Do whatever you need to do. Just take care of that cat."

In the basement, the tool room is exaggerated. The shelves. The guns. The camouflage case thicker than before, more padded, the gun heavier and the stock smoother. The cartridges brighter yellow and the copper bottoms turned to gold. I can smell the gun oil above the mold in the dank room.

I load the cartridges and snap the action shut as I walk out into the backyard.

I have some sense that I am in a city, three blocks from the University of Oregon, and I know that hunting a cat, house to house, down an alley and up a front street, is not a good idea. So I check the safety and lay my loaded gun on our deck railing. Then I go to find the cat, to bring it back to our own yard.

I search all afternoon, stalking quietly. I hop fences and creep up next to neighbors' back doors. I look under decks, in garages, behind cars. But I don't find the cat I'm looking for. There are smaller cats lounging on porches, on top of fences. Well-cared-for pets. They don't wear abscesses around their necks like wet scarves.

After two hours, I give up and climb back over our fence. Hungry and tired, I don't care about the alley cat anymore. I don't care about shooting the gun.

I walk through the backyard, up to the porch. When I get there, the gun is still on the railing, loaded and ready, with the safety on. And next to the open end of the gun's barrel, the cat is sleeping.

The alley cat I was looking for.

He is calm. When I walk up, he opens his eyes lethargically, blinking as if he has been napping for days. Waiting for me. One paw is crossed over the other, making a pillow out of his shoulder. He looks at me without lifting his head.

I can reach out and touch both the cat and the gun. But I do neither. Instead, I stand and contemplate the fact that the cat's body is three inches from the end of the barrel. I imagine what it would be like to push the safety button, to hear it click, knowing the trigger is set. Even though I've been told not to, I have dry-fired the gun many times, and I know how far the trigger depresses before it catches. Less than an eighth of an inch. I wonder what a 20-gauge bird load would do to a cat at a distance of three inches. Entrance and exit. Bones and ricochet.

I know I can't shoot an animal like that, while it sleeps on a deck railing, with a shotgun lying at its side. So I reach out and pick up the cat. I avoid touching him near his collar, not wanting to feel the wet fur. My hands wrap around his soft belly instead. He is bigger than he looks, stronger, and I realize how well he eats. His skin is warm near his heart. I can feel his lungs opening and closing. The hair on his body is cold compared to the pumping warmth of his skin. I can smell the sweet rank of his abscess. I juggle him to readjust, holding him out like a sacrifice. I don't want to bring him anywhere near my body, don't want to hold him the way I hold my own cat.

I step off the porch and set him down in the grass, then go back for the gun. I tell myself that I've made my decision. I can't hesitate or change my mind because my father does not encourage indecisiveness.

It is quiet in the yard, and still. The sound of the safety clicking off is a loud noise. I have the gun at ready position, aimed at the ground in front of me, and now I shoulder the stock, wiggling it into the front of my armpit. Adjusting. Then readjusting. I have too much time. This is not at all like the hunting I've read about in my grandfather's *Field & Stream* magazines. This is not a reflex game. It's been two and a half hours since I was told to take care of the cat.

The cat himself seems to sense no danger. He tips back on his haunches. Straightens his front legs. Extends his claws and stretches. Then he arches over, bringing his back high in the air, looking like a caricature of a cat, something a kid might draw in the margins of a book. I smile despite the circumstances. Then I press my lips together, forcing a frown, forcing my resolve. I make myself say out loud, "You scratched my little brother, cat. You hurt my baby brother."

I take a step back to gain separation. Lift the gun and center the bead of the sight just behind the front shoulder of the cat, where I imagine the heart is. The target seems bored, leaning to stretch again, yawning, sauntering toward the fence. He looks like a teenage boy coming out of a 7-Eleven. Cocky.

The cat glances twice over his shoulder as he makes his way to the edge of the yard, a distance of fifteen feet. I take a side step to keep the bead of the gun on him, still following the line of his heart.

I can smell the hexanol in the cut grass as I hold my shotgun, right index finger touching the vertical grooves of the trigger. The cat angles left at the fence, perpendicular to me. In line. The cedar slats of the fence extend to the ground where they are crossed by two-by-fours, all freshly painted white. The orange cat stands out against the white background. I can see the ends of each hair.

The cat takes ten steps along the fence. Then stops. He turns his head toward me and stares. And at this moment, he seems to finally understand.

When I was a child, my father coined the simple phrase "Hoffmeisters don't quit." It was meant to apply to music practices, soccer and baseball games, cross-country races, or difficult schoolwork. But the phrase grew. The sentence became a mantra that my closest brother, Cooper, and I said to each other before jumping off of a second-story roof into a bush or taking turns trying to shoot out a far-off neighbors' porch light with a BB gun. We said it as we swam the river in winter or beat a carp to death with a stick.

I say the phrase now three times.

"Hoffmeisters don't quit. Hoffmeisters don't quit. Hoffmeisters don't quit."

The bead at the end of the barrel begins to shake as I pronounce the words. My left shoulder cramps, and I bring my elbow into my side. I settle my right elbow as well. The cat continues to stare at me, unmoving. I think of my mother saying, "You're the man of the house now, Peter. So take care of it."

I mumble, "Hoffmeisters don't quit," one final time.

I know I have a choice but I also don't.

The hum starts. There is no voice. Only the telegraph wire of the hum, the electricity.

I make myself picture Ellis's fresh blood on the paper towel, the water thinning the color. The concentric pink circles. I picture

Ellis's tongue quivering as he cried, mouth open, two thin baby teeth coming from his bottom gumline.

I exhale and close my eyes. Then I whisper, "Don't cry, don't cry, don't cry, don't cry." I suck in breath and open my eyes. The cat is still there, fifteen feet from me, standing against the clean white fence slats.

I pull the trigger.

I tell myself that I killed the cat for Ellis, that I was protecting my baby brother. I say afterward, "It was a nasty alley cat anyway. He would've probably scratched more babies if I hadn't done it." This is how I justify.

I speak in self-defense when family members bring up the cat shooting in front of new friends or extended family. No one remembers that my mother told me to "take care of it" or that she called me "the man of the house." In my family, the motives are often taken out of stories to add conflict. According to my younger sister Haley's version of the story, the cat I killed was one of our own. But Haley doesn't know. She wasn't even there.

The story doesn't settle easily into people's minds. I am told that killing domesticated animals is often a precursor to human murder. I am played as the family psychopath. "That's just Peter," Haley says, "and he's crazy." My mother nods in agreement. I begin to wonder about myself.

I clean the fence with paper towels. I say nothing. Not aloud and not in my head. The hum is gone like a canyon broken open. Too dark to see the river.

I dig a hole under our willow tree in the soft ground, burying the remains of the cat. I don't pray for it. I don't know if I have the right to do that.

The gun is warm behind me, lying on the edge of the deck in the sun, two unused cartridges inside. I retrieve more paper towels

and a spray bottle of bleach. I wipe the fence, smearing the blood-
stain to a lighter pink. I leave extra bleach on the slats afterward,
hoping the chemical will erase the color over time.

I give the alley cat a name and burn the letters into a homemade cross at my father's workbench. I don't know then that I will
kill other animals over the next year. I will kill a family of pos-
sums with a pitchfork, a shotgun, and a shovel. I will feel nothing,
even for the babies.

And, at seventeen, in only three years, I will plan the murder
of an older boy.

I know nothing of that now. I only know that I cry, that I am
crying as I pound the cat's cross down into the earth. I drive the
wood with chopping blows, using the side of an old hammer,
rusted at its edges.

I do not cry for the cat. I do not cry for his body torn nearly in
half, for his hair and skin and flesh and nails, for his heart that is
no longer whole.

■■

CHAPTER 2

Family Science

I am six. Hillary, Cooper, Haley, and I are homeschooled, home all the time, and our mother doesn't take any medication. She is loose, as if some of her strings aren't tied correctly, lines that don't match up. This is our first year living in Tucson, having previously lived on the green tongue of an Oregon grass valley, and my mother loves the desert landscape. We comb the hardpan for her, find carcasses she can boil down into piles of bones, biologic fodder for her sculpting.

She stands in the bleach fumes in the kitchen, one of her stiff painting aprons tied around her waist, a wooden spoon dangling from her left hand like a paintbrush, telling us stories and creating names for hybrid coyotes that she'll create out of chicken wire and paper-mache.

"Aardvark and coyote: aard-ote."

"Cat and coyote: cat-ote."

"Snake and coyote: snake-ote."

She tells us that Picasso would've been just another Velázquez if he had been willing to stop at imitation. But he didn't. And Matisse extended the fauvist movement for half a century.

Our mother makes up songs with jingles and slant rhymes.

She reads us children's books: *Where the Wild Things Are, The Big Orange Splot, Bill and Pete*. She reads classics as well: *The Adventures of Tom Sawyer, The Prince and the Pauper, Arabian Nights*. She reads us the Bible. I love the way my mother reads. She does all the voices.

My mother meets a woman named Mitchel, a textile designer and antinuclear activist, a revolutionary. Mitchel has traveled around the world twice, paints African ghosts on her walls, is five feet ten and loud. She and her husband, Phin, have friends in the Guatemalan underground. When our families vacation in Puerto Peñasco, Mitchel and my mother cuddle on the porch and pretend to be lovers. My father takes pictures of the couple. We all laugh at the lesbian joke.

My mother is fun.

But we go back to Tucson, and there is another side. The color drains out of her eyes, and bags appear underneath like bruises. She blinks slowly and her voice crinkles with tinfoil at its edges.

I know what kind of day I will have by looking at my mother's face first thing in the morning. When it drops, there is nothing. We run around the desert for hours. Sometimes I am with Hillary and Cooper and Haley. Sometimes I am alone.

My mother is in the house. She will not read to us today.

My mother's parents, my grandparents, visit for Christmas. They bring Uncle Jeff, their only other child, a career special forces officer and covert operator. A ghost. He is part hero and part mystery. For my birthday he gave me a picture of himself jumping out of a B-52 into international waters. He said, "I'm this dot here," and put his index finger on the black.

For Christmas, he gives me his army-issue canteen carrier. He tells me a story that starts with "My counterpart in Thailand was saying the other day . . . "

With her family in the house, my mother is nervous. Her nervousness is like the smell of iron in the air, corrosive.

She tries to be a good hostess. She makes coffee and nice dinners. She does not paint with oils. Her current dachshund-ote sculpture sits half constructed on the kitchen counter, pushed back against the wall next to a pile of bleached rabbit skulls.

My grandparents relax all day in the living room. My grandfather tells the same stories over and over in a heavy voice. He is six feet tall, bald, and wears a mustache. His eyes never blink. Some of his stories are entertaining, stories from the wars, but others are engineering tales, math exploits from his second career as a university professor and textbook writer. During these stories, we children squirm in our seats. To her credit, my mother is patient.

My grandparents didn't attend my parents' wedding because my father had once said, "I think the Vietnam War is wrong." And that was enough to justify a boycott of their own daughter's wedding two years later.

Now, in Tucson, my grandfather is passive aggressive. "Pamela," he says, "my coffee's getting cold."

Two days into the visit, Haley goes to the hospital for croup. She spends a night in an oxygen tent, and my mother stays with her in her hospital room, unable to sleep.

The next day, my grandmother says, "Pam isn't a very good hostess. She doesn't keep our wineglasses full."

My grandfather nods in agreement. "It would be nice if she would pay attention to us."

My Uncle Jeff sits like an action figure. A small, special forces military doll. He says nothing.

It is only the third day of their visit when my mother walks out into the living room toward them. She is pushing up her sleeves, and I know the signs. But my grandparents don't. They don't know her well enough, and both of them look surprised when she begins speaking.

My mother says, "You know what? You get up and pour your own *fucking* wine! Got it?"

My grandparents don't say anything.

When we return from errands and a long dinner at a restaurant downtown, my grandparents and Uncle Jeff are gone. We won't see them again for three years.

The fight is blamed on my mother. She is at fault. She yelled at her own parents for no reason at all. She is too volatile.

When my mother was a little girl, her parents told her that she wasn't very pretty. They pointed out that she wasn't good at math and science. They said that her swimming training made her shoulders "look like a man's." They also taught her lessons such as "white people don't mix with Negroes" and "the Holocaust was not nearly as significant as people say."

Perhaps my mother's anxiety and depression are not a result of her childhood. Perhaps they are weaknesses encoded into her DNA, inevitable, determined gifts of nature. Or perhaps being told that she was ugly, unintelligent, undisciplined, and unsuccessful caused her emotions to sink, to drop into valleys, to run downhill, like water, like garbage, like cars driven off a cliff. But I am not sure. That latter is only my theory, and I am my mother's son.

I am a poor scientist.

| CHAPTER 3 |

⚏

Infection

W e go for a run.
        "Peter, I want you to do well."
"I know, Dad."
We run a half block without talking. He says, "I love you."
"Yes. I know." He does. And he always tells me.
"Good. And that's why I make you go to class every day. Every single class on time."
"Yes, Dad."

My father is involved. He comes to my sporting events. Every match, every game, every race. He's not an absentee father. He's the opposite.

He shows up to wrestling practice one day, sophomore year.

"Dad, why are you here?"

He puts his fist to his lip. Teeth tight. Flexes his hand, then points at me. "I wanted to make sure that you came to practice today."

"But I always go to practice, Dad. I don't skip."

"Well, I wasn't sure." He raises his eyebrows. "I heard that you went late to fifth period today . . . after eating lunch with a girl."

I'm fifteen and not allowed to date. I'm not sure if I'm in trouble for eating lunch with a girl or being tardy to class. Either way, I don't like him being here at practice, checking up on me. "Dad, that doesn't even make sense. One tardy isn't a skipped class. And I don't ever skip practice."

"No? Well, it's about character, Pete. Every class, every activity. On time every day. Your full effort. And who was the girl?"

"What?"

My coach steps forward, thinking he might have to separate us. "Is everything okay, guys?"

My father points at me one last time. "Every single thing matters, Pete. It's all about character."

His rules are like the edges of sheet metal, sharp and paradoxical: his liberal love combined with a rigid northern European work ethic. But my father followed his own rules, and they earned him a scholarship to Stanford. He grew up working on farms and in orchards, then in the San Joaquin Valley canneries. And he became a doctor.

On weekends, my friends and I play pickup tackle football. Coop is the only younger kid who is allowed to play with us because he's tough enough to compete with older boys. By his junior year, colleges will begin recruiting him to play defensive back.

One Saturday, my father plays too. My friends and I are excited to see how he mixes it up. We're fifteen. He's forty-five but still in excellent shape, and we want to see if we can hit like him, hit as hard as an NCAA Division I athlete. None of us have played college sports yet.

Our two teams trade touchdowns without me going head-to-head against my father. Then my team kicks off, and the ball rolls right up to him. I shade to his side and come sprinting down, imagining that I'll lay a vicious blow, imagining my father ripped off his feet, thrown wickedly to the ground. But he doesn't pick up the ball, and I slow down. He steps forward and lets it roll between his legs. Slowly. The game stops as he stands over it.

I'm in front of him. "Pick up the ball, Dad."

"No," he grins, "you can down it."

We both hesitate. The ball is between his legs. Sitting there.

The game is live but we're both standing still, waiting over the untouched ball.

"Come on, Dad. Pick it up."

"No. Go ahead and down it."

I'm confused, but I shrug and lean down to reach the ball.

My father bends with me, slowly, then tenses and swings his forearm like a short axe. I don't have time to get out of the way. My nose snaps and lodges underneath my right eye. The hit takes me off my feet, lays me on the ground. I blink. Lying on my back. My nose opens and the blood spouts over my mouth, choking me, then off the side of my face. I stand up. The blood runs down the front of my white shirt like abstract art.

My father jumps toward me and I step back wobbling. He's pointing and laughing and ready to block but I don't make contact with him. Coop picks up the ball and runs off to the left. All my friends stop playing as Coop runs for an uncontested touchdown.

My father yells, "I broke your nose! I broke your nose!" He's laughing so hard that he's hyperventilating. He jogs down the field following Cooper.

My friend Doidge says, "Man, that was fucked up."

"Yeah, whatever."

My father jogs back. "Want me to set it?"

My friends laugh at the ridiculous scene.

"I guess."

My father sets my nose at mid-field. "You're going to feel a lot of pressure, Pete." He works his thumb left to right. My septum slowly moves out from underneath my eye. He puts his right thumb opposite. Counterpresses and wiggles. Counterpresses again. He shakes his head. "You should've seen your face when I hit you. You were so surprised."

He's still smiling.

My friends shake their heads.

We keep playing. The blood on my shirt dries to a starch. When I run hard, red mist comes out of my nose.

After the game, my father buys us all ice cream at a shop two blocks away. The girl behind the counter looks uncomfortable as I pick my flavor. My shirt has a two-foot peninsula of blood down the front and my right eye is swelling shut.

In late 1946, my paternal grandmother didn't want to be pregnant for a fourth time and demonstrated her disappointment by refusing to eat more than was necessary to survive. During the pregnancy, she gained a total of four pounds. My father, large headed and runty at birth, grew to only five feet five. Smaller than his older sister, the chip of diminutive size cut like glass on my father's shoulder, he worked to become an athlete equal to his father, my grandfather, a man who wrestled and competed in gymnastics in college.

Academically, my father competed just as hard, earning perfect high school grades and the honor of class salutatorian. He credited his successes to a series of motivational lectures my grandfather delivered to him during his teenage years. So when I turned thirteen, those lectures began for me. Each night. My father's obsessive-compulsive tendencies led to one-hour, one-sided talks on the topics of homework, work ethic, discipline, and the Christian faith. The lectures' subject matter and length did not vary.

Now, at age fifteen, I can expect a lecture each night. I close my door early but I know the knock is coming. His gentle knock. His gentle tone during the lecture. Each lecture. Every night. For an hour.

While I am a sophomore at South Eugene High School—my second year in public school—an opposing coach refuses to send his top wrestler against me. After watching me all season, the coach knows I will memorize the senior's tendencies before districts, and I am given a backup as an opponent instead. I decide to punish him.

I drop the boy so hard onto his back that the referee gives me a warning. We are brought to our feet again. I look at my father in the stands. Then I lift and drop my opponent even harder, with a double-leg takedown, not considering that he might leave his knees sticking up like garden tools. I land on one of those knees, and the impact imprints a bruise on my hip the size of a cantaloupe. As I'm finishing the pin, a sack of blood is settling against my hipbone, waiting for the arrival of bacteria.

I have a low-grade fever. I win my first two matches at districts, but before the semifinals the second day, I can't loosen up. I keep jumping rope, but my muscles won't heat. I should tell my father, but I don't. Instead, I tell my assistant coach. "Something's wrong with me, Coach. I don't know what."

He looks at me and smiles. "Just win this match, and you go to state, Pete. Don't go into that consolation shit hole."

"Ok, Coach. I want to go to state."

But I don't. Not even close. I lose once, lose again, and lose a third time in the match for fifth and sixth. The only three-match losing streak of my life.

The next morning I can hardly get out of bed. When my father tells me to mow the lawn, I say, "I'm sick . . . really sick."

He looks at me and bobs his head back and forth. Touches his index finger to his thumb twice, one of his obsessive-compulsive tics. "I think you can mow one lawn, Pete. Even sick, you're an all-district athlete."

I mow the lawn and go back to bed.

Monday morning comes. My body aches in a way that makes my skin feel separated from my organs.

My father swings my door open. "Get up. Time for school, Pete."

I roll over. "I'm too sick to go, Dad."

My father snaps his fingers like a hypnotist. "Get up. All you have to do at school is *sit* through your classes. That's not even work."

I wear a loose, hooded sweatshirt so I can pull the hood over my head and sleep on my desk. I sleep through every class.

On Tuesday morning I feel as though all the strings that hold my body together are made of fuses burning down from the outside in.

School is a series of strange naps. I begin to dream. In one of my dreams, my journalism teacher comes to my desk to check on me. Normally she is a cold, severe woman. I know it is a dream because she puts her hand on my shoulder as if she doesn't care anymore whether or not my writing shows a weakness for comma splices. She says, "Are you okay?"

I whisper, "I'm too tired."

"You should go home," she says.

I don't know how I got home or what happened after school. I am at the dinner table now. The soup in front of me is red vegetable beef in big bowls. I close my eyes and think of Edgar Martinez, the great Mariners' designated hitter. He hits a double and hands me his bat. The Louisville Slugger is impossibly heavy, sticky with pine tar at the hands. I try to hold it up but am falling forward, falling again and again, and I realize that it is my own head that is too heavy now. My head feels as if everything has been pulled out and replaced by molten iron or mercury, filled and drizzling out my eyes.

Edgar Martinez swings once. Twice. Into my soup. My dream smells like soup.

I open my eyes. The candles in the center of the table have rings around them like halos. Halos silver gold. Halos crystallizing. Split fireflies. I follow a line of light to the ceiling.

My little sister Haley's face is blotchy blues and pinks put together in points like a Seurat painting. I notice pattern lines behind her on the wall. A scene in a park. Women in white dresses. Parasols.

My mother is petting my head in the car. I am crying or sweating. My face is wet. "It's gonna be okay, honey. You're gonna be okay." My mother's voice sounds strange.

The car starts to move and I close my eyes again. Sleep.

"This is going to hurt."

I open my eyes. Someone has pulled my hospital blanket down, peeled back my gown. A nurse is rubbing iodine on my right hip with a lollipop.

The doctor is explaining something. He says, " . . . to collect a sample of your bone marrow. Okay?"

I look at my mother, who is crying. I see my father on the other side of the hospital room, tapping his fingers on the bed nervously. His eyes are red too. I lift my head.

"Try to relax, Pete." My father's voice is made of cello strings.

The needle at the end of the syringe is a framing nail, and the doctor doesn't try to hide it. He puts the needle through the soft tissue above the top of my femur, covers with his hand, then leans on the syringe as he twists. Something explodes in my hip. I am sitting up. Someone pushes me back down. I can't breathe. Someone has dropped an M-80 in my hospital room bed.

The syringe dipper retracts. The doctor pulls the needle by counter-pressing with his other hand. I feel the metal squeeze out of the bone as every pore on my body opens.

The doctor flicks the syringe casing twice, shaking yellows and pinks.

"Fragment?"

"Yes, a little chip." He points. "There."

A nurse moves my IV line.

"Okay, once more."

The nurse lollipops a second time. I close my eyes. I feel the new needle start. Then the pressure and the sound of the hollow needle puncturing my bone, a sound like a switch blowing in a fuse box.

I pass out.

The bed is wet. Everything quiet. There are no doctors or nurses in the room. They are gone now. My IV beeps and I look at my parents. My mother is petting my head. She is leaned forward. I can smell her breath, coffee and lipstick.

My father is standing next to her. "You okay, Big Pete?"

"Mmm. I guess."

"You have a septic staph infection. It could've killed you in a few days."

The drugs are tunneling. My toes go away. I will be on an IV pump for six weeks. Home for a month.

Tomorrow will be my birthday. Sixteen. The age my parents will allow me to date girls.

::

CHAPTER 4

Running Away

I am five years old. Asleep. My older sister, Hillary, who never sleeps much, stands over me. She wakes me by shaking my shoulder. "Come on, Pete."

"What?"

"Come on. Crawl through the window with me."

"Why?"

"Just come on." She is two years older. Seven. She opens the window. Climbs out.

I follow her over the sill. "Where are we going?"

Hillary doesn't look back. "You'll see."

I step down onto the roof. It is a long way down. Steep. Hillary sits facing the edge. She says, "Sit and talk to me."

We're high up on the slant. I'm unsure, but Hillary is my favorite.

The first time I run away I am seven. Our family lives in northwest Tucson, in the foothills of the Santa Catalinas, on El Diablo Canyon Road. I hike more than two miles to my friend Mario Martino's house, a place where seven-year-olds are allowed to ride QuadRunners in the washes, play poker at real gaming tables, and stay up past midnight watching horror movies. I hear my parents laugh when they tell the story later. They say that any child would have left a strict home to go to a place where there were no rules.

But that wasn't the reason.

When I leave the house, sliding open my ground floor window and stepping into the desert, I have no intention of going to the Martinos'. Although I end up at my friend's house, the destination is determined after the fact. I hiked a mile along the road before I realized where I was. And I didn't leave my house after a fight or an argument. I slipped away on a quiet afternoon for no reason at all, bewildering my mother.

When I think about my childhood, I am confused. There is a lot about everything I don't understand.

I run away a second time when I am ten, from my aunt and uncle's house in Wenatchee, Washington. They live up an apple road, in a place called Pitcher Canyon. Hillary, Cooper, Haley, and I sometimes stay with them for a few days to ride motorcycles and horses, to shoot guns, to give my parents a break.

My uncle rents out a guesthouse next door to a family from his church. That family has a thirteen-year-old boy named Jimmy, who's funny and mean, a strong kid who likes to mess with younger children.

I am a nervous child. I bite my fingernails until they bleed. Pick my nose and eat the boogers. I don't work well with others, and I don't know what to do with someone like Jimmy.

He says, "I'm gonna chase you with this bamboo stick, and if I catch you, I get to beat you."

If I was smarter, I would run away. But I don't. I'm missing a sense of self-preservation. I say, "Why?"

Jimmy laughs and twirls the bamboo in his hands. "Better run, kid."

But still I don't. I've grown up in a physical family and I don't care if Jimmy's older and bigger. I pick up a metal rake and swing it at his head.

He blocks my swing, shoves me down, and beats me on the legs and back with his bamboo stick until I get to my feet again and finally run away.

I try not to cry until I'm far enough away for no one to see, but I'm running with tears coming out of my eyes. And I keep running.

There's drama in a ten-year-old leaving a place, running off and staying gone long enough to be the object of a search. But I don't think of that. I run and run, down the canyon, crying, until I'm far enough away to be alone, then I cut left into an apple orchard.

I kneel down in the grass and look at the ground, breathing hard. I pick a blade of grass and examine it, stare with my eyes as wide as they'll go, until my tears stop. Sometimes I can count away my tears in even numbers. Add tens until I get to one hundred, then count back down again. Focus so hard on the numbers in my head that I can't cry anymore. My head is still pounding from my running, my blood tapping Morse code in my temples. I count the code taps too.

I have an argument with Jimmy, who is not there. I say, "Oh, yeah? You think you can hit me? You think you can do that? You think you can beat me?"

He doesn't say anything.

"Well, you're lucky I didn't kill you with that rake. You're lucky you blocked that shot. You're just a . . . " I can't think of the right word.

I stand up and walk around. Climb and sit in the crook of a tree, looking out at the blossoms all around. My mind calms. At dusk, I climb down and go to sleep in the grass.

My uncle passes many times before I finally wake up and hear his tires on the gravel road. I stand and jog over to his blue 1970 International Scout.

It is dark.

He pushes open the passenger side door. "Get in, Pete."

When we get home, he takes out his belt. He plans to whip me, and probably should, but my aunt intervenes.

I confuse her. I watch her eyes watching my eyes. She says, "Now, wait, Tom?" her voice rising into a question at the end.

I don't tell them about Jimmy. I don't explain that running away feels normal to me.

I'm fourteen, at the end of eighth grade, the last year of home-school before I start public high school at South. Everything has changed. We don't read aloud from *The Weighty Word Book* anymore, no involved stories to learn words: *bifurcate, coruscate, ostracize, paradox*, or *quixotic*.

Hillary and I used to study Latin together at night, giggling while we translated modern phrases into a dead language.

But Hillary is in high school now. She has different homework and doesn't need to study Latin. She's found a church youth group. And I miss her. I have a hard time with transitions and change.

My mother spends more time in her studio during the day, baby Ellis playing nearby on the floor. When Ellis naps, my mother paints with oils, smokes European cigarettes, reads Dorothy Sayers novels. Her gardens are now beautiful English courtyard gardens.

My father is named the director of the neonatal intensive care unit and serves on Sacred Heart Hospital's board. He still checks my math and science homework at night but I already know how to check it myself. So we are wasting each other's time.

Our family used to scrounge together, cut each other's hair, eat "dump" dinners. My mother poured food out of a pot onto a long line of foil, and everyone ate with their hands. She used to say, "This meal is monochromatic, brought to you by the color orange." Kraft macaroni, oranges, and carrots.

But we are evolving, becoming part of the middle class. My father is not in school. We no longer collect expired food from the Safeway pallets by the loading dock. My father doesn't score Dunkin' Donuts day-olds from the bags behind the building on his way to work. There's no more Dumpster diving for fraternity furniture either. And our dining room table is a real table, not a piece of an old Lake Washington dock cut with a circular saw, bolted to two wooden sawhorses.

I am born at home, delivered by my father. I refuse to breathe deeply or cry out, staying blue long after my father slaps me on my back. My eyes look around so slow and dark and unblinking that my mother asks, "Is he retarded?"

"No," my father says, "I think he's just calm."

She looks at me again. Then she looks back at my father. "Are you sure he's not retarded?"

As I grow into boyhood, I spend most of my time alone. My mother calls me the Lone Wolf.

At the start of freshman year, I weigh 102 pounds and am new to public school. I don't cuss or wear trendy clothes. My whole identity is running cross-country, not a popular sport. But I can endure a lot of pain on the cross-country course, can push myself hard, and I'm on varsity from the first intersquad race in August, before I've attended a single high school class. I can't wait to order a letterman's jacket at the end of the season. I believe that a black letterman's jacket will give me an identity, help me to blend into the crowd.

I date a sophomore girl for a week, against the family rules—no dating until sixteen. The girl likes me because I am good at running. But she breaks up with me when she realizes that I don't know how to do anything other than hold hands. I want to have sex but I don't know how to kiss yet.

My father gets angry when he sees my midterm B in typing class. My only B.

I hate typing. I say, "Typing is ludicrous, Dad. I'll never use that skill."

"That's not the point, Peter. The point is to get the best grade out of every single class, every single term."

But typing class saves me. Mocking the typing teacher helps me to get along with the other freshmen, to get away from my homeschooled backward past. I discover this by accident. When the typing teacher, Ms. Schweppe, leaves the room one day to go to the bathroom, I say, "She reminds me of a troll."

My classmates laugh.

I draw power from that. Look around. They're watching me. I say, "She smokes and drinks coffee all day. Her teeth look like yellow piano keys."

Everyone's smiling. Everyone's listening.

I stand up, then hunch down. "She looks like this." I imitate her waddle, sticking my feet to the right and to the left at the same time. Squint my eyes and mimic her high-pitched gravelly voice. "Class, today we're going to practice using our pinkies."

Sophomore year, I start to sneak out at night. Climb down off my deck after my parents are asleep and meet my friends. We don't drink or smoke. We fight. It starts with a pair of boxing gloves that my friend Doidge bought. We box and time rounds. Fight everyone we know. Then we start to body box, bare-knuckle. We wander around looking for new people to fight.

Pretty soon, I'm fighting strangers in supermarket parking lots at one in the morning.

I run away a third time, two months after my staph infection, but this is different. This is after a fight between my mother and me.

I want to get even for everything falling apart, for what our family is going through. But I'm not sure exactly what our family is going through. I want to get even for how my parents have treated me the past two years, for how they blame their marriage problems on me, for how they've tried to cram me into Hillary's strict religious mold.

My father says, "Hillary never had any problems with these rules."

My mother raises her eyebrows and dares me to interrupt.

I shrug them off and go to my room to do push-ups. Work out my frustrations. Count the sets. They think I'm studying.

I don't study and I don't care, but my grades are hardly slipping. I have four As and two Bs.

I wrestle and run on the school teams. And that's all that matters to me. I lift weights and eat protein shakes, rotate push-ups and pull-ups every night in my room. I put twenty pounds on my frame this year, lost weight during the infection, and I'm gaining it back now.

My father says, "Peter, it's not the two Bs that matter. Bs are fine grades. It's that you're capable of all A grades, so that's what you need to get."

I can hear them in their room through the door, my parents arguing about what to do with me.

I'm sixteen at the end of sophomore year, and I don't want them anymore. My parents. I don't care if they read hundreds of books to me when I was a child and filled prayer journals with their hopes for me. I don't want them.

My mother needs respect from someone. She needs respect or the validation that she was never given by her parents. I see her neediness in her wrinkled forehead and the way she hunches forward, as if by curling her shoulders she might avoid a direct blow from her childhood.

We are upstairs in our Eugene house. I am sixteen years old and I am strong and hurt and mean. I look at her and say, "You know what, mom? You don't know anything. *Anything*. What do *you* know?"

That's all I say. But I know it is enough.

She yells, "What?" as she comes toward me. "What? What did you say?" Her voice is cracking as if her throat is coated in chalk.

I pack in Cooper's room afterward. I keep telling Cooper how much I love him. I say over and over, "I love you, Coop. I love you." There are scratches and bruises on my neck and face, and I keep fingering them, feeling the welts rise. I didn't hit her back. I didn't hit her back, but not because I am a better person. I didn't hit her back because I wanted her to know that she couldn't hurt me. Ever. I wanted her to feel powerless, as powerless as me.

Cooper is holding open the top of my backpack. He says, "I love you too, Pete. I love you too."

I stuff in T-shirts, underwear, socks, jeans, a hat, a sweatshirt, and my schoolbooks. I'm going to stay away a long time. "You *know* I love you. Right, Coop?"

Coop looks directly at me. "Yes." He brushes his hair out of his eyes. "Yes," he says again.

We can both hear our mother downstairs. We can hear her screaming that she's going to kill herself. We don't have to be down there to see the knife.

I live at four different houses that spring. The end of sophomore year. My mother spends time in the Johnson Psychiatric Unit.

| CHAPTER 5 |

▦

Church Rules

The first year in Arizona, my parents get our IQs tested. We walk into a small room, one by one, stare at patterns, answer questions, do puzzles. The test makes sense. It is a series of logical patterns. All of it. And I like working out solutions. So I know I'll do well. And I also know that my two-year-old sister Haley will do well. Four years younger than me, I've seen Haley sit on the floor and work an adult puzzle for an hour straight. Her patience and problem-solving skills are extraordinary.

My parents talk a lot about IQ before they get the results back. They tell us which famous people are known to have certain IQ scores. Politicians and actors. Athletes with especially low IQs. They explain what "brilliant" is. Mensa.

When the results come, my parents sit us all down. My father says, "Your mother and I want you to know something very important."

The four of us are listening. We nod as we're supposed to. Eight, six, four, and two years old. Blond children sitting on a tan living room carpet.

"Your mother and I want you to know that you all got the same score on the IQ test. Every single one of you. The same."

We all nod.

"Pretty interesting, huh? So you're all exactly as smart as each other. Exactly."

We all nod again.
My parents smile.
Some lies are like wax paper over a candle flame.

My parents begin talking to me about colleges. They toss around names
like Harvard, Dartmouth, Yale, and Princeton. My father says, "You
know you're smart enough to go to one of those schools, Peter. Ivy League
or Stanford."
    I am six years old. I think about it a lot. I decide that I'll go to Stanford.

I haven't been home since the fight with my mother a month ago.
When asked by an older, childless couple at a youth group event,
I answer honestly: I'm sleeping at random people's houses. On
couches. Living out of my backpack. The husband and wife look
concerned, trade glances, then offer their spare bedroom to me for
as long as I need it. So I go to live at their house. Attend school,
read, work out. A simple life.

    After a week, my father leaves a message at the house.

    When I call him back, he says, "I checked into something."

    "Yeah?"

    "Yeah. It's called Outback. Two weeks in the Colorado wilder-
ness. Following Summit."

    I pretend not to know what he's talking about, but it doesn't
work.

    "We paid for Summit, Peter. You could still go with Hillary if
you want to."

    He means the Summit Ministries camp in Manitou Springs,
Colorado, two weeks of Bible analysis, lectures, and current events
from a right-wing Christian perspective.

    "I don't know, Dad. I don't think that's going to happen now."

    I remember when our family used to be different. Subversive
Christians. When we knew that Jesus was a liberal. Our father
told us to boycott Nestlé products to support breast-feeding

African mothers. We were instructed to "be loving" rather than just say, "Jesus loves you." They had us hold signs for Jesse Jackson's Rainbow Coalition because Christians could be either Democrats or Republicans. Open-minded.

But with money has come a newfound conservatism. And Summit is part of that.

Summit was founded by Dr. David Noebel, the infamously paranoid reverend who authored *Marxist Minstrels: A Handbook on Communist Subversion of Music*.

I know Summit is the type of place they want to send me and fix me, and I see no reason to go. It's not that I don't believe in Jesus. It's that I don't believe in this new Pat Robertson version of Jesus.

When I was little, my parents had me read the books of Matthew, Mark, Luke, and John and made me memorize whole chapters. So I knew that Jesus owned only his traveling clothes, wandered from town to town, ate with prostitutes and tax collectors. And that good, loving version of Jesus was passed down from my Grandpa Hoffmeister, a Presbyterian minister and chaplain, a gentle man who never made more than eighteen thousand dollars in a year.

But my parents have faith and politics all mixed up now, a new right-wing dogma. They quote both Rush Limbaugh and Jesus in the same conversations.

I'm sitting on the floor of the youth group couple's spare bedroom as my father tells me more about Summit.

"Yeah, I don't think I'm going to do that camp, Dad."

My father pauses for a long time. "Well . . . " he says. He's not sure what to say next. He loves me, but there are the rules. He exhales. " . . . You know, if you went to Summit, you could come home afterward."

Could come home afterward. That stops me. I never considered the possibility that I wasn't allowed to come home. In fact, I thought I'd been the one who rejected my parents, not the other way around.

"Your siblings are really missing you, Pete." He always uses that word: *siblings*. I have five siblings now, including two-year-old Ellis and baby Maddie. Six kids total.

I think of the younger ones. "Yeah, I miss them too."

"Well then, you should consider it. You could come home after Summit and Outback." He says that again as though I didn't hear him the first time.

I wish I could see my father's face. Know what he's doing with his eyes and mouth. Read his expressions. But I can't. So I say, "Okay. I'll consider it."

I miss playing ghost-runner Wiffle ball and Smashball with Haley and Coop after school, miss wrestling with Ellis in the morning, miss holding baby Maddie while watching a baseball game.

I can hear my father clicking his tongue. Waiting for my answer. "Pete, let's talk next week." Now that he's played his hand, he wants to get off the phone.

"Yeah, okay."

"Bye, Pete."

I get on a plane to Colorado with Hillary, Hillary who used to be my best friend.

We spend two weeks listening to lectures and guest speakers. We become accomplices in the young religious right. As speeches are given, campers nod in agreement, take notes in spirals, break into discussion groups, pray for national Republican leaders.

This is similar to the last few years of my home life. "Love your neighbor" has been thrown out in favor of new family rules such as Christians don't celebrate Halloween, Christian teens watch "The Abortion Movie" and "The Revelations Movie," *secular* is a bad word, and Christians don't "date."

I tried to talk to Hillary about all of it, but she said, "I think the dating rule is a good rule. Christians shouldn't date anyways."

"What?"

She smiled her new condescending smile, the one that didn't exist when we were younger. "Christians should only be interested in *courting*."

I wondered where my sister had gone. The toddler who unlocked the front door at two in the morning and wandered down the street. The seven-year-old who talked Cooper and me into making the kitchen a swimming pool. The middle schooler who bought candy on the sly and resold it at a markup to younger kids.

After two weeks, Summit ends. Then I go to Outback—the wilderness experience for troubled teens. Each boy is given a backpack and a produce bag full of gorp, iodine tablets, and lemonade drink mix. We are driven to a remote drop-off in the Colorado backcountry. We backpack, rock climb, mountaineer, orienteer, and white-water raft.

Outback is my type of Christian experience. I feel closer to God outside. Like John eating locusts and honey in the wilderness. Elijah fed by the ravens. I journal and vow to work on my family relationships. I make promises to myself that I will be more flexible and compromising, more loving. I'll try to understand my parents' world view. Hillary's too. They are good people who love me. They are more conservative than me, but I will try to be respectful and love them the way I should.

When I walk off the plane in Eugene, my parents are waiting, smiling as if nothing ever happened between us last spring. I hug them. And in the car on the way home, they ask if we can go to lunch the next day and talk.

"Sure. Let's do that." I'm excited about getting time with them. Just the three of us.

"Good," my dad says, "That'll be nice."

My mother turns around in the front seat and smiles.

I sleep in my old bed that night, a bed I haven't felt for three months. It feels too good.

At lunch, my father taps the table. "Your mother and I know what you've been doing this past year." He means drinking, doing drugs, having sex. The things I haven't done that Hillary has made up.

"Really?"

"Yes."

"So you believe Hillary, huh?"

"This has nothing to do with Hillary."

"Well, that's funny because . . . " I can feel my sarcasm coming on. But I stop myself. And to be fair to Hillary, I've been wrong about her too. Made assumptions. Misunderstood her. Told lies. So I stop myself. "Okay. Forget all that. Let's move on."

"Exactly," my father says. "That's what your mother and I want. We want to move on. And that's why we've come to a decision."

"A decision?"

"Yes. We've enrolled you at Woodbridge Prep, the New York boarding school we asked you to interview with over the phone while you were at Summit."

"Enrolled me *when?*"

My parents look at each other, then back at me. "For the fall. You'll leave in a week to begin your junior year."

I try not to cry, but I start anyway. "But . . . "

My father tears up too. "Your mother and I think it's best."

I shake my head. "No. I came home because I *wanted* to be home. I *wanted* to be with my brothers and sisters. With Haley, with Cooper, with Ellis and Maddie. I went to Summit and Outback so I could come home and be with them. And I've changed. Don't you want to see that? Don't you want to see how I've changed?"

I believe that I can listen better, understand my parents more, that my change can change them.

My dad sits back.

My mother does too. Her arms are crossed. She says nothing. And she doesn't cry. She is still angry about our fight four months ago. Her parents trained her to hold grudges, and she does it well. She stays hurt. I look at her crossed forearms and tense lips and know that there is nothing I can say that will keep me in Oregon.

⊞

CHAPTER 6

Coop

S eattle. *I am nine years old. We go down to an abandoned freeway ramp that hangs over one of the side ponds off Lake Washington. From the cement guardrail to the water it is forty feet.*

My dad jumps. He hits feetfirst and stays underneath the water. He swims around below the surface, looking for obstacles. When he comes up, he yells, "It's all clear. You can jump if you want to."

Hillary and I jump. It's a long fall but it's fun. I pull in my hands and point my toes as I hit the water. Then I tread water. Look up at the bridge.

Cooper is standing on the rail. He is seven. Less than fifty pounds. Forty feet above us with a bowl haircut.

My dad yells, "Come on, Coop. You can do it."

Hillary and I chant, "Go, Coop, go! Go, Coop, go!"

I think, at first, that Cooper is hesitating because he's afraid. But when he smiles, I know he's just waiting for the right moment.

Coop says, "I burned a car last night." He says it as if he's talking about shoplifting gum from a Dari Mart.

I'm on the hallway payphone in my Woodbridge Prep dorm in New York. Fall of my junior year. "What?"

"It fucking burned and burned." Coop has just begun to use the F-word. He's in the eighth grade.

"How'd you do it?"

"Kyle and I smashed the windows, sprayed WD-40 all over the inside, and I lit it with a Bic. Oh, but I grabbed out some CDs first."

"Who's car was it?"

"I don't *fucking* know." Coop laughs as if he's on meth. He's learned to laugh like that recently too. He changes the subject. "Did you hear about Jai and Stacey, Pete?"

I nod and grip the phone tighter. "That he date-raped her?"

"Yeah." Coop pauses. "We should fuck him up."

I nod. "I thought so too."

"You know, Pete, I wish you were here . . . back home. We would fuck up Jai together if you were back home."

"Yeah, we would." I look down my dorm hallway to see if anyone is listening. "I miss you, Coop. I miss you a lot."

"Me too, man. Me too."

He seems to manufacture cool somewhere in his body. He is everything that I am not. He can wear an ugly bowl haircut, a hand-me-down sweater vest, brown shoes, black pants with a blue shirt, a Day-Glo pink baseball hat, and be at a new school to start seventh grade. Nothing matters to him. Nothing at all. Compliments settle on him like sunlight, and confidence is a process of his own photosynthesis.

Perhaps that's what scares his eighth-grade teacher.

Cooper has been at O'Hara Catholic School an entire year, long enough to be the best athlete, the boyfriend of the prettiest girl, and the leader of a gang-like following of thirteen-year-old boys. When he is voted school president at the start of eighth grade, no one is surprised. The vote isn't even close. Cooper's are triple that of the runner-up. But he never serves a day as a school representative. His teacher, Mrs. Beckendahl, intervenes.

Dowdy and churchy, Mrs. Beckendahl is afraid that Cooper holds too much sway within the local population. It is an old-fashioned power struggle. And it probably doesn't help that Cooper regards schoolwork as if it's cholera.

When my father asks Cooper what his class is reading, Cooper says, "I don't know. It's pretty boring though."

Cooper was never held to the same standards in school that I was, but my father goes through the motions. "What about your math?"

Cooper laughs. "Dad, I don't worry about math."

Strangely, until now, Cooper has held it together. He has never been in trouble at school and is rarely in trouble at home. He plays basketball with the Christian Athletes in Action postcollegiate team, even though he's only fourteen, practicing at Northwest Christian University and traveling to Mongolia on their summer mission trip. He is a 40 percent three-point shooter who prays before each game. I know. I used to share a room with him. But not now, not during eighth grade. I'm not at home anymore. I'm in New York at my new boarding school.

So I'm not there when Mrs. Beckendahl goes to the principal and has the loser of the election crowned president over Cooper. I'm not there when she singles Cooper out for academic embarrassment in front of the class, when every question he asks her results in a trip to the principal's office. I'm not there when she doesn't let him leave the class to go to the bathroom.

Cooper learns to say the phrase "Fucking *bitch*," with perfect emphasis. I hear him say it on the phone. He says it every time I talk to him.

"She's that bad, huh?"

"Yeah, she's that bad for sure. She's fucking terrible."

Perhaps a few of Cooper's past teachers considered shutting him down. It's possible. Cooper's magnetism is intimidating. But no one ever tried to destroy him until now, until eighth grade. And this teacher is successful. She cracks him.

Cooper and his best friend, Kyle, go into a bathroom at the end of lunch. There's no one in there. They tear doors off of stalls, shatter soap dispensers, and poop on the floor in front of the toilets. They paper the scene and walk out.

I stop the Big Wheel with my foot and help Cooper onto the seat. His urine-saturated diaper squishes. The front wheel is pointed down the hill. I don't think about Cooper's bare feet.

He is two and a half years old.

I pull my shoe from in front of the Big Wheel. The plastic begins to grind against the cement, sounding like a rock tumbler. Cooper and the Big Wheel grind down the hill faster and faster, arcing with the turn of the driveway. Near the bottom, Cooper puts his feet down as he has seen me do hundreds of times. He drags his soles first then the tops of his feet as he and the Big Wheel come to rest at the edge of the cross street. I go down to retrieve my bike.

I drag the Big Wheel up the hill as Cooper walks next to me. He doesn't complain. He doesn't cry. When we get to the top of the hill, to our house, Cooper continues walking into the garden and up to our mother. She's absorbed in her gardening and hasn't noticed what we're doing out front. She doesn't see Cooper's feet.

He points and says, "Oweee." His feet are raw and bleeding, tops and bottoms scraped and cut by the cement. When she doesn't look up, he says, "Oweee," again.

If I am punished for letting Cooper get hurt, then the punishment does not leave any lasting impression. But Cooper's feet do. They are crisscrossed and raw, resembling fresh hamburger, the dark lines coagulating.

◲

CHAPTER 7

Woodbridge Prep

B en, my cross-country teammate at Woodbridge, says the cook is an alcoholic. We know there is no alarm. Ben and I climb over the second floor railing.

The fourth door jiggles. It is locked like the rest, but it is loose. It can be forced. Ben throws his shoulder, popping the door, and we walk down the hall in the dark. The cook's office is the same as the outside door, locked but loose. We both push until the deadbolt rips through the skin of wood on the other side of the jamb.

I find three empties in the left side drawers. Ben finds the vodka. We put everything back into place and close the two broken doors as tightly as they will shut. Then we climb up onto the upper dorm roof.

We pass the bottle back and forth and stare out at the commons. Even in the dark, our school looks like a golf course.

I don't drink very often. I'm worried that drinking will hurt my athletics. It used to be about doing the right thing, not drinking because I wanted to be a good person. But that isn't important anymore. Nobody noticed when I made good decisions.

Ben is a senior on the team. I'm a year younger, but I run in the number one slot. He runs number two. We will both be offered college scholarships for running. We talk a lot about where we might go.

"Why do you wanna go to Bucknell, Ben?"

He shrugs. "It's my dad's school. Where'd your dad go?"

"Stanford."

"And you wanna go there?"

I take a sip of vodka. The liquor is cheap and tastes like coal. "I don't know."

Ben takes the bottle from me. "But you think you might go to Stanford?"

I say, "I don't know," again. "The wrestling coach was interested last year. My dad talked to him about me, but I was only a sophomore. The coach said that if I kept progressing, stayed clean, got a 3.5, then I could go there."

"So you still might?"

I start to shake my head no, but then I stop. "Actually, maybe."

We don't talk for a while. We share the bottle, and the vodka wiggles around the food in our stomachs. I can feel it dripping into my bloodstream. My head swells, and I roll the weight on my neck.

"Does your dad put a lot of pressure on you?" I ask.

He laughs. "Are you kidding? If I don't go to Bucknell and become a lawyer . . . " He drinks vodka as if that is an end to the sentence.

I smile, "Yeah, same."

Task-oriented, my father says, "If you're going to cry, I'll give you something to cry about." He's short, but he is strong and quick, two reasons Dick Vermeil recruited him to play tailback at Stanford.

I think I can face my father as an equal, as a man. I am twelve.

He caught me being mean to Coop. My father and I are in the back room of our new house on Moss Street in Eugene. He closes the door, giving us privacy, then pulls his belt and instructs me to come over and lie across his lap. He sits down on the couch against the wall and waits for me to do as I've been told. He holds the belt in his right hand.

All the children in our family are taught to say "Yes, Mom" and "Yes, Dad" as a reflex. We are told to speak clearly and accurately on the phone and identify ourselves when introduced to adults. We say "please" and "thank you" promptly. We are so conditioned that my youngest brother, Ellis, develops a funny tic at the age of three, an awkward string of pleases and thank-yous that make him sound even more obsessive compulsive than he already is. He says, "Please, yes please. Oh, thank you. Thanks. Thank you. I appreciate it. Thanks. Thanks." Then he smiles strangely as if he has bitten into an unripe grape.

That is how Hoffmeisters are supposed to act. Reflexive courtesy.

In the back room that day, my father waits for the cursory "Yes, Dad." He sits patiently on the couch, holding his belt, and expects me to come and take my punishment. I am a Hoffmeister.

When I say no, I see an unfamiliar look come across his face. A look of curiosity, as if he just realized that it is raining.

I am testing myself against him and I want to be clear about it. So I say, "Dad, you can't make me. I'm too old and strong now."

My father stays sitting on the couch. He chews on his lip as he stares at me. I weigh eighty pounds, exactly half of his weight, a fact I have failed to notice. Somehow, the sweat from my nightly push-ups, pull-ups, and sit-ups has bathed my brain in preadolescent confusion. I actually think I am strong enough to take on my father. I stand and glare at him.

Ben and I are on a mileage run out by the sound. A river dumps there, a cold and fast coastal channel. We take off our shoes to wade and swim across. We can cut our ten-miler down to an eight-miler by swimming the river.

We wade in next to each other. Ben says, "You know that girl Mallory?"

"Not really."

"She's the one with the black Mohawk."

"Oh, yeah." The school didn't let her keep the Mohawk, but everyone knows her by that feature anyway.

Ben rubs his naked arms. "I think she's fine."

"Really?" I feel the water above my knees as I step forward.

"Yeah, check her out some time. She *is* fine. Her hair's still fucked up. It's growing out and everything, but it doesn't matter."

"Really?"

"Yeah, really. I mean her head looks like it has a roadkilled skunk on it, but she's still hot. How many girls can you say that about?"

I hold my shoes above my head. "Hmm. I don't know." I start swimming.

Ben follows me.

Ben is dating Mallory by that weekend. As far as school friends and teammates go, Ben and I are good friends. We hang out every day for three months. We run together, lift weights together, drink together. I go to his home in Kennebunk, Maine, for Thanksgiving.

Ben is dating Mallory, so I hang out with both of them. And Ben's right. Mallory is fine. She's messed up and fine. She's a drug-addicted, sad, drunk, pretty girl. And smart.

I get in the back of one of our friend's cars on a Friday night. He's driving us over to the SUNY dorms, a half mile away, for a quick liquor run. I don't know that Mallory will be in the back seat, on the other side. And Ben isn't there.

I try not to pay too much attention to Mallory. I turn to the driver as I shut my door. "Hey, what're we going for?"

"Hard A. Any kinda fifth."

I nod. "Alright. I know some guys. Go to the end dorms over there."

We drive down the Woodbridge Prep entrance road.

Mallory giggles. She is halfway through a punk phase, still wearing black but with a grown-out Mohawk. Her girly giggle doesn't fit her appearance.

When we get to the dorms, the driver says, "We'll wait for you here." He hands me thirty dollars. "Try to get something good. But whatever, ya know. Alcohol's alcohol."

"Okay." I reach for the door handle.

Mallory slides over against me smelling like lavender shampoo and cigarettes. She has a raspy little girl voice. "Get something good, Pete. Get a lot." Her hand drops onto my thigh, fingers on the inside. I know that her hand is there as an alcoholic, as someone who needs to get drunk. But I can't help hesitating.

I am at Villa Academy for fourth grade, the only grade-school year that I attend a real school. The Villa girls who look cute to me don't like me. The girls who aren't cute don't like me either. No one likes me. Not even the boys who I beat in football and soccer. It doesn't matter that I am a good athlete. Or good at school. The teacher has me teach math lessons to the class because I am two grades ahead. She has me teach class as she sits at her desk and clicks her red Lee press-on nails on her desktop. My teaching of the class only makes things worse. Kids don't look me in the eyes after that. I return to my desk and pick my nose, rub the corners of my eyes until they turn raw and pink, tap my index fingers against my thumbs, count four up, four down. One, two, three, four. Four, three, two, one. Counting. The counting makes me feel better.

We're all out on the playground playing tag at recess, and no one chases me because they don't want me to be it. They don't want me to touch them.

Mallory is wearing a black baby-doll dress. Short. Her high-lace combat boots make her legs look better than they are. The straps of her dress are falling off her shoulders, sliding away from her collar-bones. She is looking at me with her blue lupine eyes, her face six inches from mine. I tell myself to get out of the car. She is dating my friend and not me and I am nine years old again, the new kid at a Catholic grammar school. I have a haircut that was never in style and a black beret on my head. I am sitting in the back of my fourth-grade class. I will stay back there until I learn the currency of cool, whatever it is I do not have.

| CHAPTER 8 |

▪▪

Cross-Country

The wall is a machine, my bedroom humming, electric lines strung over my bed. I know I am alone and I won't scream.

The wall is moving machine parts again, chutes and bearings, tubes and slots and gears. I am sitting up, my comforter hanging across my thighs, goosebumps spiking out from my bones.

Eight years old, I sleep by myself. In the old house in Seattle, there is no one downstairs except for me. The floorboards under my feet are cold and worn. I curl my toes, scraping my nails across the grains of the hardwood. I can hear the scrapings like a layer added in a symphony, my toenails, the wooden slats, and the sound of the machine making the rhythm. The clickings and slidings and changing gears do not bother me. But the humming stays. The baseline humming breathes, the continuous exhale of a sleeping man. I will break, or I will fall into that exhale like a person falls forward into water. When the sound does not change, I give myself to the humming. I nod forward, slipping down as if I am falling asleep in a full bathtub.

At night when I am alone, the machine comes suddenly like an old relative. The machine moves in, settles, unpacks its suitcases in the closet, hangs coats on the bedroom hooks. The machine moves in with its monotone.

Once the machine and the hum are established, the voice comes after.

*The voice demands. Calm. Insistent. No eight-year-old can stay a
child against the will of such a voice. So I do not remain a child. I become
the wolf.*

*I change my breathing to match the hum. Tap my fingertips with my
thumbs. Close my eyes.*

The voice is so calm.

Move your pillow to the floor.

I move my pillow to the floor.

At Woodbridge, I have a work-study scholarship to run cross-
country in the fall, wrestle in the winter, run track in the spring.
The school wants me to win a state title.

Officially, my work-study job is aide to the athletic director.
The athletic director's name is Mr. Thomas. I go into his office in
the athletic department each day, sit down, and do my homework.
That's my job. Sometimes I drink water or coffee out of a Styro-
foam cup. Other top athletes have similar jobs.

Mr. Thomas is a huge animal, 260 pounds of former college
wrestler and football defensive lineman at the University of Mary-
land. He coaches football, wrestling, and lacrosse in addition
to directing athletics and seems happy with his position at the
school. His wife is the choir and theater teacher. They have three
boys.

Mr. Thomas and I get along well. I will be his top wrestler in
the winter.

When I arrive at the athletic department each day, Mr. Thomas
says, "Make sure you study hard. Don't fall behind on your books."

"Yes, sir." I smile and sit down and look forward to wrestling
season. Sometimes he and I talk about my weight or about my
running and lifting.

One day, Mr. Thomas comes out as I'm studying. He sits down
next to me in a chair that seems too small to accommodate him.
He leans forward. "So what would you say to joining the football
team?"

"Football? Next year? Yeah, I might do that."

"No, I meant this year."

It's a month into the football and cross-country seasons. I say, "No, cross-country's going well for me. I'll go to state for sure. Maybe do well there."

I can tell Mr. Thomas doesn't get told no very often. "No?" he says sarcastically. "No? You don't think it would help you get ready for wrestling season?"

"Uh." I can see I've made him mad. I've misjudged him. Spoken too quickly, like joking with a new friend. I say, "Well, I don't know actually. Let me think about it a little bit."

"Yeah, you do that"—Mr. Thomas's tone is odd—"and I've got some work for you to do today."

I try not to look surprised. He's never had me do any work before. As I copy letters and fold them into envelopes, I consider Mr. Thomas's demand.

The next day, I tell him that I have a chance to win state in cross-country. It's the truth. I'm being recruited by colleges already, and Woodbridge Prep is only a Class C high school. I really could win state as a junior. Definitely as a senior. I've beaten some of the best runners in the state already.

Mr. Thomas rubs the top of his head with one of his hands, a hand that is the size of an outfielder's glove. "So you're saying that you won't play football for me?"

I planned on this question. "Actually, I'm not saying no. I'll probably play next year. But this year I want to see how cross-country finishes up."

"Hmm," Mr. Thomas moves a stack of papers. He picks them up and slams them down. "I need you to clean and organize this desk."

A week later, I hurt myself. I'm stupid. I wrestle one of the football team's linebackers in the hallway, a kid who tries an awkward choke as both of us are falling to the ground. When I plant my hand on the floor, arm straight, my collarbone comes out of joint and collapses on top of my right lung. The injury feels as if I am burning a hole in my chest with a heated fireplace poker. The ambulance takes me to the emergency room a half hour later, and a doctor puts the collarbone back in place by rolling my hand and popping my shoulder.

The orthopedist I am referred to says, "Wrestling is out for this year. Your collarbone joint won't heal well enough to withstand repetitive jarring." He prescribes Percocet and naproxen sodium. I bite my lip but don't feel it.

Mr. Thomas smirks. Then he takes me off my job as aide to the athletic director. He has me transferred to dish duty. My right arm is in a sling. In the heavy steam from the 180-degree water, I sweat as I move dish racks around with my one good arm. After a few days, my sling begins to stink like the dish room. Old gravy and Thousand Island dressing. I can smell it in class.

Ben washes dishes with me. "Fuck Thomas. He's an asshole."

"Yeah, pretty much." I grunt as I slide a rack of plates into the dishwasher.

"Who does he think he is?" Ben reaches and puts the rack in for me. Then he goes back to washing his pots.

"I don't know, man." I shake my head.

I have a different workout schedule after that. I lift lower body until I can swing my arms again, then I train with modified workouts. When my collarbone heals enough to sprint, I run speed intervals to catch up. I am focused. Healthy enough to run the last four dual meets. I win every single one. At a tristate invitational before the league meet, against the best runners from New York, Pennsylvania, and Connecticut, I place seventeenth, clocking 15:44 over a rolling 5K course. Fifth out of New York runners. And still a month to go until state. I'm catching up now. I think I can drop twenty seconds and win it all.

But Ben is gaining on me. The weeks I missed have narrowed our gap, and by championship season, he and I are close. At the league championships, Ben finishes a few seconds behind me. At the county championships, I stress out and fall apart at the end. Bad strategy and bad race management. I slip from first to third in the last fifty meters. The defending county champ wins. Ben finishes second. He has finally beaten me. And for some reason, that bothers me more than losing the county title.

I have to beat Ben at state. I want to win the title as well, but I have to beat Ben. I run on my own between county and state, opposite practice times from my team, training harder than I should. I lift in the abandoned weight room by the track. I do extra sets and think about winning state. I know that losing the county race was a fluke. I was ranked number one. I'd beaten the defending county champ earlier in the season, beaten him by twenty-eight seconds in a dual meet.

Even though training myself into the ground the week before state is not recommended, I feel as if I have to punish myself for losing county, that I have to punish myself for losing to Ben. And I have to do it alone.

When the team gets their state jerseys from the athletic department, I'm not with them. I'm off doing my own workout again.

When I see my coach later, he says, "Go in and get your state jersey, Peter. Someone will be in there still."

I walk toward the athletic department. It's evening in early November, getting cold, dark already.

Most of the lights are out in the athletic building. One office was open though, Mr. Thomas's.

I hesitate.

"Mr. Thomas?" I knock apologetically. Quietly.

"Yes?"

"Mr. Thomas, could I get my state jersey from you . . . please?"

He scooches his chair back and stares at me. He looks enormous even in a seated position, like one of the Roman army's paid giants. But he smiles. "Sure."

I follow him down the front hall, then a second hallway, then down the back stairs. The lights below us aren't on. He doesn't reach for the switch, and we turn left into the darkness. I follow him. A few steps down that hallway, he flips on the lights. I can see the old shower room at the end of the hall, the outline of the tiled doorway.

We stop at the equipment room. Mr. Thomas fumbles with his keys, then opens the door. I relax when he turns on the final set of lights. I didn't realize that I'd been holding my breath.

Mr. Thomas goes over to a bin marked x-COUNTRY. He looks at the tags and finds a medium. He hands it to me, navy blue and smooth. Then he finds matching shorts.

I take those too. "Thank you."

"Do you want to try the jersey on?"

I don't want to, not right then. But the question makes sense. "Okay. Yeah."

Mr. Thomas stands in the doorway, waiting for me.

I strip off my shirt and slip the jersey on. It's tight, but fine. Tight means no wind drag. "It's good," I mumble.

Mr. Thomas is still standing in the doorway, leaning against the jamb. "Will the shorts fit?"

I glance at him quickly. I say, "Um, yeah. I've been running in the same size all season. This size." I fold the uniform once, on the bench, and put my T-shirt back on. I grab the gear and start toward the door without looking up. Then I stop.

Mr. Thomas is still there. He's in the doorway, leaning casually, smugly, looking amused.

"Uh, should we go, Mr. Thomas?"

"Hmm?" His left hand is in his pocket, and his right arm hangs long and thick from its contact point with the door, at his shoulder. I look at that big, loose right hand. I stare at it.

"Should we go?" I am still looking at his hand.

The index finger and thumb touch once, quickly. Then I look up at his face. Mr. Thomas is smiling. "Go?" he says. "Well, I was wondering about something actually."

"Uh huh?" I don't know whether to step back or sit down on the nearest bench. I feel thickening. Claustrophobia. I can hear it in my ears.

"So your coach told you to come get your state jersey?"

"Yes."

He asks again, "He told you to?"

I start to bob my head. Not in the way that means yes, but in the way that means I need to leave now. I almost forget to respond. Then I say yes again. A third time.

"So he told you?"

"What?" It's in my ears loud now. My right hand is turning into a fist. I am two steps away from Mr. Thomas.

"So he told you to come down here after hours and pick up your jersey?"

I say, "What? Yes. Coach told me to come get it." I can feel the sweat on my palms now as I tighten my fists then release them.

Mr. Thomas is still leaning, leaning heavily, leaning as if he might lean the wall down. He takes up the whole doorway. His navy-blue collared Woodbridge Prep Football shirt is untucked, bulging over his belly, tight around his biceps. The shirt is coming unseamed at his shoulders. Mr. Thomas shakes his head no. He smells like bad coffee. "No. You know what I think?"

I have to get out of this room. I have to get out of this room right now. "What." I spit the word at him. Quick. I take a half step closer.

He blinks slowly, for effect, to bother me, to show me that he will never move and we will never leave and we will always be in this room, in this basement, with him blocking the doorway.

He says again, "You know what I think?"

I don't answer him. I've started to tap my fingers. I can feel the adrenaline dripping in my heart.

Mr. Thomas says, "I think your coach didn't tell you to come down here. I think you're a liar."

I feel the rush of his words, feel them mix with the hum in my ears. And then I have a thought and I smile wildly. I know my way out. I know my way out of this room.

"Well you know what, Mr. Thomas? I think you're a fat fucking piece of shit."

That loosens him from the doorway. That breaks his casual lean. He pulls his left hand from its pocket and reaches for me. I duck but Mr. Thomas's overhand right catches me on the top of my back, near my neck, and it chops me to the floor.

I get up swinging furiously, one, two, three, four, but I connect only with his stomach and ribs. He knocks me to the floor again. Then his hands bunch up my T-shirt, tighten the cloth around my throat and chest, and I feel myself being dragged out of the doorway and down the hall.

I get my feet under me once more but Mr. Thomas knocks me down again. He drags me on my knees down the hall toward the shower room. I fight his grip, his hands. I tear at them, scratch at them, but they are big and thick and strong, and my T-shirt is wound up inside his fists, wound up like bailing wire around a fence post, and I can't get clear.

I swing my feet around and pop up one last time, but Mr. Thomas easily throws me down in the corner of the hallway and continues to drag me. We are close now, close to the end of the hallway, to the shower room and the tiles and the dark.

All of a sudden there is screaming in the hallway and there is someone else on top of me, sprawled on me, then pulling me up, pushing me back against the wall. I see the face of one of my dormmates, a friend, Mike Hoskins, a linebacker on the football team. He is yelling, "Be cool, Pete! Be cool!"

Another of our dormmates, Hanif Granville, dreadlocked and enormous, a football player and wrestler, has Mr. Thomas backed up against the opposite wall. "Chill, Coach! Just chill!" Hanif has no shirt on, and he's pointing with his sharp index finger at Mr. Thomas's eye socket as if he might gouge that eye out.

Mike grabs my face in his hands. "Let's get outta here, Pete! Come on, man!" He says it as if he's seen everything, as if he understands everything that has gone down.

"Okay," I nod. "Okay."

When I look back, Hanif is still talking into Thomas's face with that finger pointed like an ice pick.

I don't report the incident. Mike and Hanif don't either. We understand the established power structure, what might happen, what would happen. A tenured faculty member's word against three work-study kids, two of them black. So none of us even try.

Mr. Thomas tells a different version of the story. He tells a tale of staying late at work, being asked to do a favor, questioning what I said, and being cussed at in return. Thomas doesn't say anything about a fight.

I receive two demerit hours for swearing at a faculty member. I shovel leaves as penance on Saturday morning.

The faculty wonders what is wrong with me. Why would I swear at a teacher? Am I different than I seem? Are there other faults that they've missed?

My English teacher gives me demerit hours for forgetting to shave on a Tuesday morning. He says, "I noticed that you are a little lax about your personal appearance, Mr. Hoffmeister. Let's take better care of ourselves."

My dorm dean gives me two hours for my "tie being too loose" on Thursday. I realize that they are cracking down, putting me in my place, making sure I'm not headed in the wrong direction.

Another dean notices that my shirt is too loose at school the next Monday. He says it is "almost untucked" and gives me two more hours. They're helping me develop character, catching me before I become a lost sheep.

I earn four more hours, then eight, then twelve. The leaves turn to snow.

My cross-country team goes upstate for the championships. It's the first time in many years that the team has qualified, and my teammates are excited. But on the bus to the motel, I keep thinking that I don't care. I don't care at all.

My coach, Mr. Lingle, notices how quiet I am. "Are you okay, Peter?"

"Yeah, I'm fine, Coach."

"Hmm," he puts his hand on my shoulder. "Stay focused. Remember to be conservative at the start." He knows what he's talking about. He used to hold the world record in the indoor mile. "Conservative," he repeats. "Just go out slow. Run it like an accelerator."

"I know, Coach."

I want to look him in the eye, tell him that I appreciate him, his kindness, but I don't say it. I'm feeling guilty already. Guilty for the failure I'll be on the course tomorrow. I already know I won't race well because running isn't important anymore.

He still has his hand on my shoulder. "Whatever's going on, Peter, don't let it get to you. You'll regret it. Just run your own race. And remember to go out slow." He takes his hand away and stands there for a minute, in the aisle, looking at me, then moves back up to his seat.

The next morning, on the line, it is four degrees Fahrenheit. I didn't warm up well and I tell myself that it's because of the cold. I make excuses. And at the gun I start off hard. Go out fast. Run with the lead pack for the first mile even though that isn't the plan for me, and not a good plan at all. I usually win if I go out slow. I lose if I go out fast. So when I begin to drop off the pace running up a long, steady hill, when the leaders surge and I don't stay with them, it's not a surprise to me.

I step off the course right there. On the hill. I walk off into the woods and watch the rest of the runners stream by. One hundred and fifty pass me while I'm standing in the woods. Then I walk back to find my coach.

By late November, my demerit hours stand at twenty-three. I am working toward an unofficial record.

I go home with Ben for Thanksgiving in Maine. I tell him what happened with Mr. Thomas.

He says, "We should tell my dad. He's a lawyer."

"Yeah, maybe. I'll think about it."

Ben and I get drunk instead. The next night we throw a rod in his Jeep, totaling the car his father loaned us. That is enough for his father to deal with. So we don't bother him with the story of Mr. Thomas and me.

Back at school, I don't care anymore. I let it go. Let everything go. I earn demerit hours on purpose. I feel in control if I do that. I don't shave, then stroke my cheeks in history class, pretending it's an absentminded action. I wear my tie inside out. I leave my shirt untucked. I have fifty-seven hours by Christmas. I work after school Monday through Saturday all December. My shoulders and arms are strong from shoveling snow.

⬛

CHAPTER 9

Christmas

I sneak out one night during Christmas break. Back in Eugene. Home from Woodbridge Prep. Before I arrived, my parents decided that my friends were the problem, so they said that I couldn't leave the house without a parent or Hillary as a chaperone. Sixteen years old, I am stuck inside for fifteen days straight. Tearing my fingernails off. On the last night home, I crawl out the back of the house and meet my friends.

Doidge and I hit the 7-Eleven for a beer run. He and I have both started drinking more, and he suggests that stealing is easier than shoulder-tapping.

I say, "Whatever. It makes no difference to me."

He smiles and holds the door. I run the beer.

Our friend Mike drives getaway and stalls the borrowed car twice. But he figures out the stick shift well enough to get us to Washburn Park.

The night is cold and clear, hooded-sweatshirt weather, and we shuffle our numb feet as we guzzle Budweisers and tell stories. Doidge and I drink most of the case. I walk home around 5:00 AM, climb back up onto the high porch, and sneak into my room.

My father wakes me an hour later. We have a family Bible

study. I burp loudly and my family looks at me as if they don't know what's wrong with me. That's all I remember. When it is over, I go back to bed.

At 10:00 AM, three hours before my flight back to New York, my father tries to wake me up again. I am passed out.

My father throws me in the shower in my clothes.

Hillary is there. She keeps saying, "Peter, you're embarrassing our family. *You* are embarrassing our family."

When I get out of the shower, my father is standing in the hallway, shaking my driver's license in front of my face. "You're losing this for sixth months. You might not ever get it back."

I laugh. I'm drunk. And I'm going back to a boarding school in New York where I have no car.

Hillary reenters the scene. "The younger kids are gone. We sent them to a friend's so they wouldn't see you like this."

"We?" I ask.

Hillary snorts at me. She and my father are indistinguishable.

"What if the kids had *seen* you like this?"

"Do you know what *you're* doing to this family?"

"You're going to be *sorry* about this later."

My mother is in her room.

There is a storm over Long Island that night. Thunder and lightning hit just outside of LaGuardia. The puddle jumper pitches heavily in the darkness, dropping thirty feet at a time, bouncing right then left. I am sorry. My hangover is mature by then. I'm sorry about my headache. I'm sorry about my nausea. I'm sorry that I don't have a beer to settle my stomach.

In three weeks I will walk away from Woodbridge Prep. I will walk out of the headmaster's office into the most perfect snow I have ever seen. The whole world will be bleached clean white.

■

Selling Ben Out

When I sell Ben out at Woodbridge Prep, it goes like this: We were at the river by the sound. Ben said that he thought Mallory's hair looked like a dead skunk's. Ben and I both laughed. It was a little thing.

Ben started dating Mallory, and I became friends with her too. Mallory and I hung out alone one night without Ben.

The next day, Ben looked worried. He said, "What happened, man?"

"Nothing. Nothing at all." It was the truth. Mallory didn't like me like that.

"Are you sure?"

I said, "Yeah, man. Nothing happened. Nothing at all."

Then Mallory and I hung out alone again. I didn't tell Ben and he didn't find out.

I began to wonder why Mallory liked Ben and not me. I thought about Mallory when I walked to class. When I lifted weights. When I lay in bed.

Mallory and I began to hang out a lot. Drink together. Talk about our families.

I didn't think about Ben at all.

One night in January at SUNY, across the street from Woodbridge Prep, I remembered what Ben had said about Mallory months back. The little thing I could make big.

I look at Mallory. Right at her. And I think about Mallory and me. Together.

"You know what Ben said about you?"

We're sitting on a bench closed in by a bamboo break. Mallory is awkwardly swinging her legs. She says, "No. What?"

"He said you look like a roadkilled skunk, that your hair's all fucked up."

"Did he say anything else?" Mallory takes a nervous drag on her cigarette. She looks like a black-and-white picture of Manhattan.

"Ben was laughing his ass off. That's all I know."

I don't tell her that I was laughing my ass off too.

I stare off. "Yeah, he said your hair looked fucked up. I remember that. He said *fucked up*."

Mallory turns quickly. "Did he say *I* was fucked up?"

I hesitate so she has to wonder. "No . . . " I shake my head slowly, as if it's hard to remember. "I don't think he said *you* were fucked up. No, he probably didn't say that."

Mallory taps her cigarette filter against her lip.

I am a bad person.

CHAPTER 11

Expelled

My demerit count stands at eighty-eight hours even before I go into Bar and Pete's room. I'm not good friends with either of them, but Pete and I hang out sometimes. Pete is the headmaster's nephew, a midyear transfer from a prep school in South Carolina. He plays football and lacrosse, wears his shirt and tie with the casual sloppiness of a boarding school lifer. And like most lifers, he doesn't care much for rules.

I hear muffled whispers through the door, then explosions of laughter. I knock. There's a bump and then the room gets silent.

The door cracks open. Pete's face appears. He smiles and turns to the people behind the door, "It's cool. It's only fucking Pete Hoff."

Everyone inside the room laughs. Pete and Pete. A good joke.

"Come on in, man. Come on in."

I walk in and set my books down. School's just out. Everyone is huddled by the open window. It's cold. Below us, three stories down, kids are shuffling across the street toward the dorms. The lower-school kids, the eighth graders and freshmen, have the farthest to go from their classrooms. They're moving slowly on the January sheet ice.

Bar leans forward. He's holding a .22-caliber, double-CO_2 pellet pistol. He whispers, "You gotta hit 'em in the coat, in the chest, where they got a lot of padding . . . "

Someone else says, "Get 'em, Bar."

Bar steadies his right wrist with his left hand. He squints and pulls the trigger. It makes a little pop sound. We all lean forward to see who's hit. A freshman named Saul grabs his chest, rocks twice, then falls down on his backpack.

We drop to the floor. Silent. Then somebody starts giggling. And everyone begins laughing. It's wrong. We know it. But it's too funny. We all laugh as if we're watching a horror movie.

One of the other boys in the room, a kid named Jeremy, says, "Hey, hey. I wanna shoot too. Lemme have a turn. Lemme have a turn." He's a snob from the other dorm. Not an athlete, not on scholarship. Jeremy's an academic, and he's rich.

Bar hands him the pellet gun. "Go ahead, man."

"Yeah, go ahead, man." The group encourages him.

Jeremy steps up to the window. His gun hand is shaky. He's not coordinated. But he has a gun now. It's *Lord of the Flies*. He looks like Jack after Jack stole Piggy's glasses.

Jeremy rests his shaky hand on the windowsill. He screws up one cheek to close an eye, to aim. Then he pulls the trigger. An eighth grader takes it in the shoulder and whips around in a circle before falling down. We drop to the floor again. It was a bad shot, but we cackle like the hunters.

Pete takes a turn. Then Evan. Then Thomas.

Then I say, "Okay, my turn." I want to show that I'm a good shot. I want to make somebody fall down.

Thomas hands me the gun.

The group huddles up around the window.

"Come on, Pete."

"Shoot somebody, Pete."

I aim carefully. Evan and Thomas each missed their first shots. I don't want to miss at all. I aim carefully at a freshman I don't know. He has just stepped onto the sidewalk below, shuffling his leather shoes on the ice. I aim for his thickly padded chest, where his sweater and coat puff between the two straps of his backpack. He has his thumbs hooked behind the straps, and I aim at the invisible line between his thumbs.

Then I squeeze.

Pop.

I watch the freshman go down hard. Then I duck. We all cover our mouths with our hands but our laughter is still loud. I'm laughing so hard that I'm shaking. I'm shaking and holding the pistol.

I sit up. "I wanna go again."

I shoot two more underclassmen. Then someone grabs the gun from me.

We all take turns that first day.

Before we leave the room, Jeremy says, "We should do this again tomorrow, right after school. Meet here."

Bar nods. He's holding the pistol. "Okay. But don't tell anyone."

We meet up to shoot again the next day. And the next. A Friday. Three days in a row. If the day after that wasn't a Saturday, we would have kept going. We are that stupid. All of us. I am stupid. I don't think about it at all over the weekend. I never even consider getting in trouble.

By Monday afternoon, rumors come from the student council meeting. A freshman boy's ear has been torn by a pellet. The pellet went right through, tearing an uneven hole the size of a pencil's eraser. The parents of the boy are preparing a lawsuit and calling for the expulsion and arrest of the shooter.

We meet in Bar's room. Bar speaks first. "Don't say *shit* to anybody. Anybody. What happened in here is our secret. If we don't talk, they can't figure anything out."

Pete steps forward. "Yeah, we gotta keep quiet, guys. Real quiet. My uncle's pissed." No one knows if his uncle being the headmaster will make things better or worse for us.

I see Jeremy's face. He looks as if he's going to cry. He mumbles, "I can't get caught for this."

We all turn on him.

Pete says, "Fuck you, man! *No one* can get caught for this!"

Jeremy shrinks back. "No . . . I just . . . I mean I really can't get caught for this. I'm going to Yale."

I laugh at him. "Have you never been in trouble before?" I am becoming cocky about my demerit hours, about my reputation. Everyone knows how much trouble I'm in.

The group laughs with me. We're scared. We have to laugh.

Pete gets invited over to his uncle's house that night. We wait nervously in the dorm, pretending to do our English and history homework.

Pete comes to my room afterward. "Can I talk to you a second?"

"Yeah, I wasn't really studying." I am holding *Paradise Lost* but I'm fifty pages behind.

My roommate, Dan Cortez, is studying at his desk behind me.

Pete points at Dan. "Should we talk alone?"

"No," I say. "Dan's cool. He knows."

Pete purses his lips while he straightens his tie in the mirror.

I wait.

Pete turns toward me. "It's not good, man. My uncle already has your name."

"*Has* my name?"

"Yes, *has* . . . or *had*."

I toss *Paradise Lost* onto my bunk. "You mean that he *guessed* my name?"

"What?"

"You mean that he *guessed* my name because I have a lot of demerits?"

Pete shakes his head. "No. He said he knew you were a shooter."

"What? But nobody else? How's that even possible?"

Pete shrugs and holds up his palms.

I shake my head. "But it's *your* room. Did he say he knew you were in on it too then?"

"No. He said you must've borrowed Bar's pellet gun and shot kids before we got back to our room from school."

"But that doesn't even make any sense. How could I get in?"

"We could've left it unlocked." Pete sighs. "That's just what he thinks."

I look around my dirty room as if searching for a response. Dan beats me to it. He's been pretending to study until now. Dan says, "Fuck that and fuck you, Pete Basinius! You let that shit go? You didn't straighten your uncle out?"

Dan's wiser than me.

Pete shakes his head no.

But I let him off. I say, "Fuck it."

Pete mumbles, "I heard it's only gonna be a three-week suspension . . . "

Dan is disgusted. "Fuck you, Basinius."

Dan's right. He's right and he's loyal. But for some reason I care too much about what Pete thinks.

Pete looks at me. "What do you think, man?"

I say, "I think it's bullshit," but I don't say anything else. I'm already letting Pete get away with it. A suspension doesn't sound too bad. And I'll get to go home. I'll get to see my brothers and sisters.

Pete's nervous. He doesn't know me well enough to trust me. He says, "So should I have volunteered the information my uncle didn't even know?"

Dan looks right at him. "Yes. You should have, Pete, you fucking loser."

Pete puts up his hands. "But we promised not to say anything . . . "

"Shut up," I snap. Pete's standing there with his casually wrinkled clothes and his family money and his unbrushed hair. I hate him. But I also want to be him. I say, "If you're so afraid, Pete, then fuck you. And fuck it. I don't care."

"What do you mean?" Pete isn't defending himself. He knows he has no character to defend in this situation. He only wants to know if I'll take the blame.

I roll my neck. I'm tired. But I can play the self-righteous victim. As if I didn't shoot anyone myself, I say, "I'll take three weeks off for you, you fucking cowards."

Pete exhales in relief. That's all he wants to hear. "Dude, I'm really sorry about this. We'll make it up to you. Thanks so much for . . ."

Dan stops him, "I believe we said to shut the fuck up."

"Yeah," I agree with Dan, my loyal roommate.

Pete leaves the room.

Dan shakes his head. He points at my chest. "What the fuck, man? You should've fucking beat that kid's ass."

"Fuck him. Fuck all of them." I open up *Paradise Lost* again, trying to find the right page.

But Dan is right. I should've done something. Anything. If I wasn't a coward, and a needy coward at that. If I didn't care too much what people think.

Not until the middle of the day on Tuesday do I know what's really going down. My cross-country coach, Mr. Lingle, corrects my misconceptions. "You *will* get expelled, Peter."

"Are you sure, Coach?"

Mr. Lingle puts a paternal hand on my shoulder. He's a good man, and he's sad for me. "I'm quite sure, Peter. There's no three-week suspension for something like this. You *will* get expelled."

I call a meeting with the other ten boys right after school. Everyone is there. They all want to know what I'm going to say.

When we have the door locked and a towel stuffed into the crack, I say, "Okay, look. Here it is: Originally, it looked like a three-week suspension. And I could handle that. But now I've been told by a faculty member that I'll get expelled. And I don't know if that's true. I don't know if I'll actually get expelled, but I know there's a definite chance. So what do you guys think?"

I wait for someone to say something, to step up, to volunteer in any way.

No one says a word.

Bar shifts back and forth on his heels. It is his gun and his room and he says nothing.

Pete bites at one of his fingernails. It is his room too. The shooters are all in his room.

I look around the circle. No one looks back at me. Heads down.

Jeremy begins to cry. "I just can't, guys. I can't. My parents'll kill me. And I'm going to Yale."

One of the other boys agrees, "Yeah, we won't get into college, man. And you're already in trouble so . . . "

"Shut up." I point at them. "I could give you all up, list off all your names."

That gets their attention.

But I don't want to give them up. I want to be the kid who takes all the blame. I've started to like being in trouble, taking all the punishment and all the glory that goes with it. It is self-righteousness and social cowardice in combination. But there are limits to the punishment I'll accept. I know there's no glory in disappearing forever.

So I say, "Here's the deal. I want to take the blame, but Pete is the headmaster's nephew. If we all come forward together, the headmaster won't expel eleven students, especially not if one of them is his nephew. We'll all get suspensions, not expulsions. People will admire us when we get back, and we'll be known as the shooters. Maybe even looked up to. Trust me. What do you think?"

I see that Pete wants to volunteer. He looks around the circle once. He wants to do the right thing. But today is not the day. He looks back down again.

The island is burning.

Jeremy is still crying.

I turn on him, "What the fuck are you crying about? Do you

know what I'm doing for you?" My self-righteousness is reaching a ridiculous pitch.

No matter how many goals I score for the team, I will never be a hero. Sports can't save me. My clothes are hand-me-downs and my haircut is wrong. I don't know how to play Nintendo. I am the smallest fifth grader in the sports camp. Sixty-two pounds.

I have a ten-year-old's notion of war. Trench to trench. But shooting and killing won't save me. I think I have to die for someone else. For the sacrifice. Selfish sacrifice. For the glory of it.

My dorm dean warns me after dinner that I will, for sure, be expelled in the morning. I thank him for the warning. Pete Basinius comes to my room at lights-out. Dan says, "Get the fuck out, Judas."

I am a fool, though. I still care what Pete thinks. "What's up?"

Pete smiles. His hair is casually greasy. "Come down to my room. I've got beer for us."

Dan looks at me unbelieving as I throw on a hooded sweatshirt. I creep down the hall to the big corner room. The room where we shot the pellet gun.

Bar has gone home for the night. Pete has all the lights on in his room as if he doesn't have to follow rules.

I sit down on the floor next to the bunk beds. Pete pulls a twelve-pack of MGD cans from under his desk. He rips open the cardboard and lays a can on the floor. He rolls it to me. I field the can and pop the tab. I chug half the beer and sigh.

Pete is at the CD player. "I'll play you something I listened to my last night at my old school." He clicks buttons, programming repeat.

I chug the rest of the warm beer. Pete rolls me a second.

The music starts and Pete sits down on the floor by his desk with his own beer. He and Bar have the biggest room in the dorm, three times the size of mine. There is a comfortable gap between me and Pete.

R.E.M.'s "Everybody Hurts" begins to play on the CD player.

Pete and I talk about the song. We talk about girls we think are fine. We don't talk about the pellet gun or his uncle or the expulsion hearing. That's all over now.

The expulsion hearing is a mock trial. Pete's uncle looks me in the eyes and explains what I have done. He propagates the obvious lie that Pete and Bar were not involved in any way. I have been told, before this meeting, that the headmaster was a decorated colonel in the army in his previous career, that he was a man of great character. But it's difficult to believe.

One of his many leading questions: "So you broke into Mr. Basinius's and Mr. Musof's room, found Mr. Musof's pellet gun, and shot fellow students without Mr. Basinius or Mr. Musof having any knowledge of your actions?"

I try not to smile or laugh or cry. I want to do all three.

I say, "Yes."

When the headmaster likens my actions to the massacre at Mi Lai, I do finally smile. The hearing has become a good joke. The headmaster is a good joke.

I am nobody's hero. I'm a good joke too.

The school will supposedly box up and send everything I don't take now.

I pack the things I care about, what I don't want to be stolen by the other boys on my floor. I know that it will be the richest boys who will steal the most. Not Dan. He won't steal. But Pete and Bar will. Their friends.

My dorm dean hands me my plane ticket at the taxi. "Good luck, Peter."

"Thanks." I shake his hand.

The ticket is a one-way from LaGuardia. I hope the final destination is Portland or Eugene. I want to go home. See my family. See Cooper and Haley. Maddie and Ellis. But I'm not going back to Oregon. The ticket says Tucson. I'm going to stay with friends of the family.

▦

CHAPTER 12

The Letter

I have a picture of it. The Kodak date is July 1984. My mother looks thin and maternal in her baggy art school clothes. She has her hand on my back. She is wearing sunglasses. I am dressed in a blue button-down shirt. Seven years old. Cooper is almost five. He is looking up at me, wearing little-boy red suspenders.

I have a cigarette between my index and middle finger. I am mid drag. Cooper is waiting his turn. We are smoking cigarettes with my mother. We are smoking European cigarettes because smoking European cigarettes makes us artists like Picasso.

Next year we will smoke again, after my mother and father have heard of a new parenting technique. My parents will make us smoke until we throw up. Cooper and I don't know that yet. When the picture is taken, it is still early in the smoking process. Cooper and I look content. We are learning. We are trying new things. Hoffmeisters try new things. Hoffmeisters don't quit.

I want to make a small wood fire on the patio next to the pool, add sage and juniper boughs, cleanse myself with smoke. But I have no traditions and this is not my home. My parents want me to write a letter.

My parents arrive in Tucson a week after I get expelled from Woodbridge Prep. At the airport, my mother's mouth is tight at the edges. My father is nervous and obsessive about small details, like how he moves his fingers.

Cooper will be expelled from O'Hara Catholic School in a week and they just spent two days negotiating with O'Hara's headmaster and Cooper's eighth-grade teacher, trying to work out a compromise.

Over the past two years, I have told a few lies about my parents, sometimes to protect them and sometimes to hurt them. I have told more truths, but my parents' rigorous pursuit of perfection is shattered by both fiction and nonfiction alike. Any negative is family blasphemy. Honesty is to be sacrificed for positive public image.

And so there is the letter idea, and the idea is simple. Simplistic. I will write a letter announcing that every negative thing I have ever said about my parents is a lie. Every single thing. Then I will photocopy the letter twenty-five times, sign the bottom of each letter, and send the copies to my friends and acquaintances back in Eugene.

The idea is so ridiculous that I laugh. I'm starting to wonder why everything is like this.

I know I need to stop. Stop everything. Say no. Tell the truth. Always. Start making better decisions. I feel as if I've chosen to walk through a bad carnival, past crooked mirrors and games with impossible odds. I should stop, but I keep laughing.

My father leans forward on the opposite couch and snaps his fingers. "Do you think this is a joke, Peter? Do you think getting expelled from high school is a joke?"

I stop smiling. "No, I don't."

My mother's arms are still crossed. She looks small and tight and angry. She looks unfit to operate a motor vehicle.

"Peter, you're *going* to write this letter," my father says.

I should say no. What could they do? But I say, "Okay. I'll write the letter."

There are two authors: my father and my mother. Then there's a scribe: me. I hold the pen as my father remembers specific statements he wants refuted. My mother adds terse interjections. I don't argue at all. I write whatever they say.

When we finish, we read it over together. It's not a letter. It's a half-true confessional.

My father says, "Good."

My mother says, "Mmm hmm," and nods.

We make twenty-five copies at the Circle K down the street. The copies are poor and I sign the bottom with a signature that is nothing like my own.

My parents smile.

Next, we come up with the names of recipients. I name all my close friends. I'm not worried about them being fooled by the letter. They'll know that it isn't written by me. They'll know that it isn't my voice on those pages. But after I name my friends, my parents write down a list of random people I used to know a long time ago, then a list of very obscure acquaintances.

I say, "Won't those people be confused? I mean, I don't even talk to them. I haven't said any of this to them. Ever." I point to a couple names my parents have written down.

My parents glare at me. They don't respond to my question.

"Okay," I shrug. "Let's send it to them. All of them. Fine by me."

When we finish placing stamps on the sealed envelopes and drop them in a blue box, my mother's shoulders lower. She hugs me. My father stops moving around so quickly. At some point after my expulsion, my parents developed the letter plan, and now the plan has been completed. They can relax. They have gained a small measure of control over their son who is difficult.

| CHAPTER 13 |

■■

Tennessee

I don't talk to any other students for two weeks after I arrive at Lion's Gate School in Seymour, Tennessee. Early February of junior year. I'm almost seventeen. I don't need new friends.

During class I am quiet. At night, I go up to the headmaster's house and sit in his living room with him and his wife. It is odd, but I like them. The headmaster's name is Mr. Bean, and he says, "I'm going to be a mentor to you." We drink glasses of sweet tea and talk about books, history, politics. For some reason, I am comfortable here.

Then Mr. Bean is fired. The Baptist board votes unanimously against him, leveling the charge of "progressive liberalism." And that is it. He is finished. Lion's Gate School is a historically proud, conservative reform and college prep school in East Tennessee, and the board has no desire to see the school evolve into an eastern-style boarding school.

Mr. Grubb, the board's chairman, comes in as the new head-master. Like other Southern Baptist headmasters, Grubb is rigid and mustached. He means to change boys like me. He tells me that the first time I meet him.

"Mr. Hoffmeister," he says, "I know what kind of young man you've been before."

"Sir?"

"Yes. I know. And I *will* change you."

Two weeks have passed and Mr. Bean has already moved out of the state.

Lion's Gate School touts itself as a college-prep boarding school first and a reform school second. That's the school's advertisement. But my dorm looks like a mental hospital: cement floors and hallways, metal doors, bars, screens covering exterior Plexiglass windows.

My new dormmates have committed misdemeanors and felonies, have been expelled from schools, have dealt drugs, deal drugs, don't study, don't read, can't read, are gang members, and never planned on going to college in the first place. I'm in the middle. I like to read and read well, but I have one high school expulsion on my record.

The only time my mother visits Lion's Gate, she tries for the entire day not to cry. I can see it in her tight cheeks like sunburn. She tells me later that she cried the whole evening after she left.

It is a Friday night after lights-out when someone knocks on my door.

I unlock and crack it.

A head slides in. Greasy hair like a fifties movie. "Hey, man, I'm James. Come outside and give me some advice, huh?"

James is our Cassidy. Known as a boy who can steal a car, seduce a girl, or make up a song in thirty seconds. He is thin and tall with big feet and long, awkward hands.

"What?" I say to him. "Go outside?" I've never actually met James until now.

"Yeah. You're Pete, right? Want to come or what?"

I hesitate. "I don't know. It's after hours, man. Is Steve gonna unlock the door for us?" Steve is the on-duty dorm dean.

James squints at me as if I'm retarded. "Steve? Oh, hell no. But he don't need to unlock nothing for us."

I slip on my shoes. I'm curious.

James walks down the hall like a boy who's used to being in trouble. He doesn't slink along or look back or hush me. He strides to the stairwell and jogs down the stairs. His feet make confident noise, as if he knows exactly how many decibels he can produce without getting caught.

The basement of our dorm is a combined laundry room and lounge, six coin-operated Kenmores sitting across from two orange couches. Past the couches, at the east end, there is a push-latch door, the institutional kind you might see in a business building. Everyone knows that the door is tied to the fire alarm. Pushing the latch at any time causes a dorm-wide ring, everyone awake, a trip to the headmaster's office in the morning. But James walks right up to the door, reaches to the top of the jam, and slides something in the space as if pushing a debit card into an ATM machine. Then he messes with a wire on the left side.

He's done this before. "That'll work," he says.

I nod. "Oh."

James pushes slowly on the door's crossbar and eases it open. No alarm. We each scrape through. Then James pulls a small wooden triangle out of his pocket to wedge the door open behind us.

He whispers, "Nothing like pulling something off in juvi, then getting locked out on the return, huh?"

I nod again.

Because I arrived midyear, a month after the start of second semester, everyone assumes I came from a juvenile detention center, the common scenario for midsemester transfers. The story going around school is that I shot someone in the head. No explanation of the gun or the injury caused. It only matters that I shot someone in the head. So it is generally assumed that I am on parole. And I don't correct the misconceptions, because at Lion's it is good to be mysterious and even better to be feared.

James and I walk down to the Civil War memorial. The memorial is a stone wall, ten feet high and two hundred feet long, abutting the football field. James climbs the side and pulls himself up. I follow. The wall is four feet wide on top, like a medieval barrier, and we sit down comfortably, a few feet away from each other.

"You smoke, Pete?"

I shake my head.

"Went to juvi and didn't pick up smoking?"

I smile at the thought of all my nonexistent days in juvi. "Nope," I say.

James is looking at my shoes. He seems to pick up on everything, examine every detail. He pulls a cigarette from his pack with his teeth and lights it, then stares up at the sky. "I need some help," he says, and exhales.

"Yeah?"

He closes his eyes and takes a drag, bobbing his head. "Yeah."

I extend my legs and bend to touch my toes. I have a nervous habit of stretching my hamstrings around strangers.

James blows a large smoke ring, letting it sit in front of his face, then a smaller ring to send through the first. His smoking makes me think of endless hours alone.

James smiles. "PO's been killing me." He squints his eyes. "Stepfather too . . . So I gotta get outta here, go some place."

I wrap my fingers over the ends of my toes, head down. I look up. "Where are you gonna go, man?"

He waves his cigarette hand in front of his face as if he's shooing away a fly. "Somewhere good. San Francisco maybe." He says the name as though it's a magical city in a storybook.

"Oh." I've been to San Francisco. To me it's a real place that I didn't love. "You have family there?"

James laughs. "No."

I go back to stretching my hamstrings.

James lies down flat, smoking and staring at the sky.

I lean back too. The sky is still cloudy. There hasn't been a star in the sky for days.

James says, "I could hitchhike there in less than a week."

"A week." I repeat the phrase out loud as if I am doing a math problem, stalling to think. I say, "Does it ever rain here or just stay cloudy all the time?"

"Oh, it'll rain," James says. "You'll see. It's gonna flood."

We could keep walking. But my sister Hillary clearly said no before he fondled her.

I step up and drop him to the ground. I'm only fifteen. It's luck. He is bigger than me, but I came from behind where he couldn't see me and I hit him in the ribs. I stand over him as if I am going to kill him with my hands.

I never see his friends. One of them has a dirty cast on his arm that leaves a crisscross mark below my nose.

I curl up on the concrete and hope they won't hit me anymore. I keep my face down in my own pool of blood.

The ambulance driver and the paramedics say we shouldn't go to the hospital in that part of town.

The floods come the next week. The sky opens as if God slit the clouds with a box knife.

Steve takes a group of athletes on a run before school. Steve was a medic in the navy before he became a dorm dean, and he calls the run "a hardening exercise." But most of us actually like it.

We run out south of the school on a single-lane highway. One of the boys will die in a car accident on this road in four months, but none of us know that then. The flood rains have been going all night, and the dips in the road are ponds straight across. We run downhill into the flats, a series of fields, fenced-off rectangular lakes on our left and right. The road dips for twenty feet, all under water. I look at the faces of the other boys. Happiness and exertion. Working hard against heavy shoes.

I am the only track athlete in the group, so I take the lead, push the pace, and open up a gap in front. Chris Fowler, a point guard on the basketball team, stays close. I hammer on the upswellings, then cruise down into the water on the other side. At the bottom of one of those arcs, I lose the road.

I've been running for thirty seconds through water up to my shins when I notice that everything in front of me is a level lake of muddy-brown water, fence posts dotting the surface at odd angles. The lines of the fencing no longer match up with my idea of the road. Then I step off into the deep water. I don't even know there's a river until I am swimming.

I come up. I know I have to swim hard or I might get stuck against a barbwire fence like a dog caught in a flash flood. I can see the top lines of the field barriers, sagging strings of metal everywhere.

I spin around, treading water, trying not to be frantic. But I was breathing hard before I fell in the water.

I gulp at the air. Push and paddle. Spin. No road.

Then I see Fowler. He's behind me, yelling to me, cupping his hands around his mouth like a swim coach. I can't hear what he's saying, but I can see that he's standing on the road with the water just to his knees. So I put my head down and swim to the side, angling toward him. I touch mud a foot under the water, scramble and slip along the bank, and crawl until I reach the road. Fowler steps over and holds out his hand. I grab his wrist and he pulls me up.

We both stand at the edge of the road, the start of the river, the water pulling against our calves like a riptide.

"Fuck," I mutter.

"Yeah, fuck that," Fowler says.

Neither of us tell Steve about my swim. Boys at our school don't tell adults anything.

Across the hall from me in our dorm, Fowler lives in a double room. Fowler is chubby and strong, deceptively good at basketball. He can beat me easily in one-on-one. Pale white, with thick acne, he comes from a part of Knoxville where no other white people have ever lived. He loves the NBA and hip-hop and knows every underground rapper in the South. We sit on his floor at night listening to demos and bootlegs. We do push-ups and joke about drinking. We tell stories about our friends back home.

Sometimes a senior named Levi walks into Fowler's room. Levi is soft and big, nervously tucks his shirt in underneath his gut while he talks. When he wipes his nose with the back of his hand, his glasses go crooked and he reminds me of a copier repairman. I don't know why. He's constantly saying, "Y'all know that the Christian thing to do is . . . " He's capable of finishing that sentence a hundred different ways.

There is a girl who Levi is obsessed with. She is a year younger than me, a sophomore. Levi tells us that their families are friends and that everyone wants them to get married. I look at a picture of the girl that Levi carries around in his wallet, and I know immediately that the marriage is never going to happen. But Fowler and I put up with Levi talking on and on about her, about how beautiful she is, and how virtuous, and how she'll make an ideal wife. The funny thing about all that is that Fowler tells me she's engaged to some nineteen-year-old who already graduated a year ago. The girl wears an engagement ring on her left hand. And she doesn't seem virtuous at all.

But I have my own charade going. I've been telling people that I'm dating Mallory. It's easier that way. She calls every week and sends me letters too. She writes that she loves me now that I am gone. We never dated in New York, not even close, but now we talk all the time. Fowler spreads the story that I have a girlfriend. And I never correct him.

The first time Fowler and I drink mouthwash, we don't plan to. I'm messing with the toiletries on top of his dresser and I pick up the bottle. Off-brand mint Scope from Walmart. I turn the bottle to read the ingredients. "You know what would fuck us up, Fowler?"

He raises his eyebrows. "Huh?"

I shake the bottle. "This mouthwash."

Fowler giggles. "Shit, Pete. Probably so."

"Yeah, 40 percent alcohol. Says right here."

Fowler is lying on the floor, switching CDs. He props himself up on his elbow. He says, "You think it'd hurt us though?"

I shrug. "Fuck if I know. But there's Robitussin drunk, NyQuil drunk, probably a lot of other drunks too. So mouthwash drunk?"

"Huh . . . "

I unscrew the child-safety cap and smell the contents as if I've never smelled mouthwash before. Under new circumstances, it smells quite different, more pungent, overwhelming. I say, "Yeah, I don't know, man."

Fowler stands up and takes the bottle from me. He smells it once, twice. He squints one eye shut. "Maybe . . . "

I take the bottle back before he can try a drink. I like to go first. I shake my head, exhale, and tip the bottle. I have no intention of sipping. Either get drunk or don't drink. I chug eight or ten ounces in four gulps. Then I lower the bottle and choke. Hold back a retch. Tighten my stomach.

"Dang, psycho! What the hell." Fowler grabs the bottle from me. He nods and swirls the contents. "I'm with you, man." He chugs even more than I did and sets the open bottle back on the desk.

We both stand, panting like big dogs on a summer day.

I sit down. Fowler sits down next to me.

"You feel alright, Fowler?"

"It burns like shit, man."

"Yeah, me too."

Fowler grins and I can see the saliva pooling in his mouth. My saliva is gushing too and I'm pretty sure I'm going to throw up. "We better go down to the bathroom and puke down there."

"Yeah, probably."

We hurry down the hall into the bathroom.

We hang out over the urinals as if we're pee shy. I drool a continuous string into the catchall at the bottom, my mouth open and oozing long strands down onto the pink urinal mint. But I don't throw up. After a while, my head begins to roll loosely and my saliva stops. I put my head against the wall. Feel the cool tiles against my forehead. I stop sweating.

I forget Fowler is there next to me until he says, "You drunk as fuck, Pete?"

I laugh. "I guess so."

Fowler spits hard into the urinal. "Yeah, me too."

■

CHAPTER 14

Chung Seoul

I don't think much of him at first. I notice him though. He makes everyone notice him. He's always doing his Tae Kwon Do forms in the dorm hallway to show off, talking loudly about his second-degree black belt. My old friend in New York, Jeong Heok, had four black belts and stabbed a man to death in a city park with a scuba knife. So Chung Seoul's martial arts and loud bragging don't impress me.

Chung Seoul is one of those boys who wants everyone to be afraid of him. He's transplanted to Tennessee from Los Angeles and wears a big, stupid Raiders Starter jacket. He wears it every time we leave school, even when it's a hot, muggy, Southern day.

Chung Seoul likes to show people the bullet in his leg.

We're on a weekend hike in the Smoky Mountains with our dorm dean Steve. Chung Seoul's in the back, smoking Marlboro Reds, making a face as if he just got poked in the eye with a sharp stick. He thinks that squinted-up face is badass.

He motions to me with his cigarette butt when we stop in front of a small waterfall. "You ever seen shit like this, man?" His English sounds like Korean-Latino English.

"A waterfall?"

He pulls up his pant leg a little higher. I hadn't noticed it before. He gestures toward his leg. "No, man. Gang shit, uh?"

The bullet is small and blue underneath his skin, next to his tibia.

"It looks really small. Is that a .22 bullet?" I use my best scientist's voice.

Chung Seoul nods seriously. "Yeah, I could have died, no?"

I shake my head and look perplexed. "From a .22 bullet under the skin on your leg? No."

Another boy who is listening starts to laugh.

Chung Seoul looks at me as if he wants to put his cigarette out on my face. Then he snorts. "They were shooting at me with Glock 9s and shit too, man. And Berettas. You know what that shit is like, uh?" He grips my shoulder.

I keep my smile but I don't look him in the eye. As much as I wish I were, I've never been shot at. The other boy stops laughing too.

Chung Seoul's hand is still on my shoulder. "You're a real smartass, *tong seng*."

I know *tong seng* means "little brother" in Korean, and I don't like the way Chung Seoul says it. But I let it go. I don't like his tone and I don't like him but I don't do anything. I tell myself that it's because I can't afford to get in trouble at a new school. That's why I let it go.

Back at school, Chung Seoul won't leave me alone. He knows he's gained an advantage. He calls me *tong seng* all the time, in the dorm, in class, smiling with his eyes even when he doesn't smile with his mouth.

One night as I come out of the bathroom, he says, "Oh, little *tong seng*," and ruffles my hair as I pass him.

I turn around and step into him. All the boys around us stop. They circled up. They know what's coming.

We're eye-to-eye. Chung Seoul has a wide scar at the top of his left cheek. We breathe into each other's faces. I can smell the kimchi on his breath. If I start, just start immediately, then there will be no fear. None. Then it will be quick. Hard. Ten seconds. Twenty maybe.

But I hesitate. I don't know why. I don't start. Don't swing. I just look him in the eye. Hesitate. It's my turn and everyone in the hallway knows it's my turn. I have to make the decision. Chung Seoul has made it mine. But I do nothing. Nothing at all. I stare. Keep staring and waiting as if I've never been here before.

I forget myself.

Boys are circled up and I continue to hesitate.

Then Chung Seoul says, "Goodnight, *tong seng*." Winks and turns. Goes into his bedroom.

I still have my fists clenched like a fool. Boys shake their heads and go back to their rooms.

I promise myself that I will take the next chance. If I do, I'll be able to end it. That's what I think. Everything will be fine.

We have a submission fight night in Fowler's room. It's informal, on a Friday, when the dorm deans won't come down to check whether we're doing our homework. It begins with Fowler and his roommate, Jamie, wrestling on the cement floor. Jamie taps Fowler with a front choke. Then I fight a kid named Paul who is big and soft and uncoordinated.

Chung Seoul walks into the room like a middleweight champion. He flicks his chin in my direction. "*Tong seng* can't do that to me."

I stand up quickly. "Come on then, Chung Seoul. Come on."

Chung Seoul rolls his neck and shoulders, beginning to warm up. But I'm already stepping toward him. Starting it. He has no warm-up and he telegraphs a spin kick. I catch his leg, a trap in a single-leg takedown. Then I kick in his other leg like breaking kindling. His head goes down toward the corner of the room and I take the leg I'm holding and try to crush his whole body into that angled, concrete space. I jump on him and force his head into the corner where the cement walls meet the floor. I grab his throat with my open left hand and beat his head into the corner with my fist. His eyes are closed but his mouth is open, and I punch like trying to crack a watermelon with a crescent wrench.

Fowler and Jamie pull me off.

"Holy fuck!" Jaime is pulling me by my shirt.

Fowler has his arms around my waist. "Easy, psycho! Easy. Were you trying to kill him?"

I don't say anything. I let them pull me off and stare at Chung Seoul, who is holding his hands over his face.

He rolls awkwardly to a sitting position. His face is sticky. He rubs his eyes with the palms of his hands. Then he blinks, red at the outside corner of each eye. He jumps to his feet and runs out of the room.

"Damn!" Jamie says. "You weren't kidding around there, Pete."

"Not with him," I laugh. "Fuck him."

Fowler says, "Yeah, true. But, man . . . "

I think it's over. I think I'm not afraid anymore.

| CHAPTER 15 |

◫

Tong Seng

Exactly twelve months after the staph infection, there's
something wrong with me again.

I beg Steve to take me to the hospital. For two days I lie in my
bed at Lion's Gate, curled in a ball, trying to find a position where
the stabbing in my gut will not be so severe. Steve comes into my
room the second day and tells me I have food poisoning. He calls
on his military medic experience.

"Pete, you need an enema."

I say, "No. I don't think so," but he jerks me off the bed, pushes
me onto the floor, and pulls down my pants. I curl into a fetal
position. The concrete smells like rain as Steve performs medicine.

I barely make it down the hallway to the bathroom, where
everything in my bowels explodes into the dorm toilet. I stumble
back up the hall to my room. Delirious. Doubled over. The pain
in my gut is worse than before.

"Steve?"

Steve is gone.

I lie down on my bed again. "Someone?" I yell. "Help. I need to
go to the hospital . . . Someone?"

Nothing.

"Anybody? Hello?" I'm yelling from my bed, out my door into the empty hall. I lay my head back on the pillow. I don't think I can get up again.

I yell randomly all afternoon but there is no one in the dorm. I hear my calls echo down the dorm hall, off the wall. That evening, when a kid finds me screaming in my room, he goes to look for Steve. But after half an hour, he returns and shakes his head. "Man, I can't find nobody, Pete. I'll tell 'em when I see 'em though."

Later that night, he finds the other dorm dean, Jeff, who loads me into his Chevy Malibu and drives me to the children's hospital in Knoxville. We park two blocks from the emergency room entrance. I force my feet to work as we walk up the hill together. I tell myself that I only have to make it to the entrance. I only have to get to the entrance and someone will help me.

When the first ER nurse sees my face, she runs for help. I am in surgery in less than five minutes.

It is only an appendix. I am fortunate that an appendix oversight does not kill a person in two days. I am fortunate at the beginning and the end of my sixteenth year. I come out of surgery four days before my seventeenth birthday.

I play soccer that spring because Lion's Gate has illegally recruited nine exchange students from Brazil, Japan, England, and Wales and needs two Americans to fill the gaps. I'm not that good but I make the team as a stopper. I work hard at practice, put in extra work afterward, and I'm tired every single night.

I come into my room one evening before dinner. Exhausted from running ball-handling drills, lines, lifting weights for an hour afterward. My jersey is in my hand, soaked. Sweat drips off my shaved head. The dorm hall light hasn't been turned on yet and my soccer cleats echo against the walls in the near dark. My door is open an inch, nothing new because I usually forget to lock

it. I step inside to reach for the light. That's when I smell some
thing. Body odor.

I hesitate, scanning the room. Someone is in there. I flip the
light on, and there is Chung Seoul, standing next to my desk. He
says, "Come in."

I can't think of anything else to do, so I enter and close the door.
Try to seem nonchalant. When Chung Seoul steps toward me, I
sidestep him and sit down on the bed.

"You know what?" I fake a yawn, "I don't really wanna hang
out right now."

"Hang out, *tong seng?*"

"Yeah, I don't feel like it. I'm tired."

Chung Seoul squints his scar up next to his eye. "I don't care
about that, *tong seng.* You disrespected me."

I throw my shirt at the chair by the door and miss. Then I look
at Chung Seoul. He's high. Cranked. The twitching in his cheeks
looks like bugs under his skin. So James has sold to everyone now.

I feel tired. At a disadvantage. I don't want to fight Chung
Seoul. I don't want to fight him when he's cranked up and I'm so
tired. I just shake my head. "I'm not going to fight you, man."

"No, *tong seng?* You won't fight me?"

"No."

"'Cause I'm going to fucking teach you a lesson, uh?" He rubs
the knuckles of his fist against his own hip. He flexes his hands.

I scoot back against the wall. I feel like a sixth grader caught
stealing from an eighth grader's backpack.

Chung Seoul cracks his neck both ways. "You told people that
you don't like me."

I lie. "No, I didn't."

"They said you think I'm a fool."

True. I'd used that exact word: *fool.* "No, Chung Seoul. I didn't
say that."

Chung Seoul cracks his knuckles and licks his lips, the taste of
speed froth. "I'm not going to let my fucking *tong seng* talk about
me like that."

I can smell his body odor. I think I can smell the chipped white speed on his breath, and I know I can't fight him. My fear is in. The fight in Fowler's room disappears. It never happened. I'm too afraid and I hate Chung Seoul. I hate him. And I hate myself. But I'm afraid.

Chung Seoul sees my fear. His lip curls. "So you are my little *tong seng* again, huh? *Tong seng*, ya?"

I resent this, all of this, but I can't make myself get up off of the bed. I can't. I'm sitting on the bed, slid back, back against the wall. My feet are out straight, off the floor, like a grade-schooler's.

I give in. "Yes."

"My *tong seng?*"

"Yes."

Chung Seoul ushers me into his room the next morning right before breakfast. He drapes his arm over my shoulders.

"Here you go, *tong seng*, you take these." He puts four white pills into my hand.

I don't ask what they are. I swallow them right there, dry. "Thanks."

"Of course, *tong seng*. Of course."

Later, during math class, while my desk, my calculator, and the whole room feel static against the ends of my fingers, Chung Seoul runs his fingers through my hair from behind. I jump and hit my knee on the underside of the desk.

He laughs and whispers, "Feels electric and shit, huh?"

I wonder if it would feel electric and shit to break his mouth, to snap his top row of teeth off with my fist. I wonder if it would feel electric and shit like beating a dog to death with my bare hands.

I can't sleep. There's the humming. I sit up, thinking about family, wondering how Coop and Haley are, and the little kids. The yellow streetlight from the turnaround comes through the gaps in my window screen like shards of loneliness.

I am returning from practice again, tired, my shin guards flipped down. My cleats clunk along the floor.

"*Tong seng*, come into my room."

I shake my head no. "Gotta shower, man."

He wiggles his finger. "Come in one minute, uh?"

I shake my head again but say, "Okay."

Chung Seoul is doing dips between two chairs. He has his shirt off and I can see his homemade tattoos, Korean characters I can't read and a 4 LIFE cliché in Old English lettering on his stomach. Chung Seoul looks strong. He is working out more than anyone right then. We all know each other's habits.

"You want more speed, uh, *tong seng*?" He is high again.

It's evening. I feel like sleeping. But I mumble, "Sure."

He bottles out a few more pills into the palm of my hand that is white like surrender.

James takes the mouthwash bottle from me and drinks a couple of ounces. He sucks at the mint aftertaste. "Shit, man. Ain't bad."

"Yeah," I nod, "not too bad."

The mouthwash *is* that bad, but it's 80 proof and $2.29 a bottle at Walmart.

James takes another swig and passes it back to me.

I drink. Wait. Burp carbonated mint liquor. "You still going to San Francisco?"

He wags his head back and forth, drunk. "Oh, hell yeah."

I take another drink. My stomach feels as if I've lit a sparkler and shoved it down my throat. "When?"

"Another week. I'm gonna need your help. You still down to work on Steve when I go?"

"No problem, James. No problem at all."

In the dark. The cement is cool on my hands as I drip invisible sweat to the floor. It is better to do push-ups in the middle of the night than to lie awake with regret.

I do a set. Then rest flat on the floor. Arms outstretched.

I do another set. Rest again.

A third.

My boxers are soaked. I remember being the smallest kid in class. I may as well be small now. My chest gives out during the fourth set.

Chung Seoul keeps doing his Tae Kwon Do forms in the hallway. He has plenty of space inside his room, between his desk and his bed, but he does the forms where everyone can see. He's lost it now. He lifts weights every day as if he's shooting 'roids. But he's junked on speed. Somehow it works. It doesn't make him scrawny. I don't know how. He looks powerful. He tells me one night that he wants to rape a girl at our school. He tells me his whole plan as he does handstand push-ups against the wall, his body upside down.

I start thinking about how I beat him in that fight a month earlier, smashed his head into the corner and punched him until Fowler and Jaime pulled me off. I remember it every time I pass his room. I remember it when I run lines at practice. I remember it when I lift weights afterward. Then I go back to the dorm and sit in his room before dinner, talk to him as if he's my older brother, a mentor, my best friend. He tells me stories about L.A., about his gang, about fights and guns and girls he's fucked. He tells me how he'd hold girls down and do whatever he wanted to them. He laughs as he imitates their screams.

And I listen.

I trade him in lies. Lies about Tucson, Eugene, New York. I tell detailed stories going back to my childhood, made-up stories, gangster fairy tales. And when I make up something particularly violent, Chung Seoul nods and smiles. "That's good, *tong seng*. Uh? That's good." He likes the dark stories the best.

The truth was violent too. But not in ways that would have made sense to Chung Seoul. I was an obsessive-compulsive child who often hurt people on accident.

At sports camp. Fifth grade. I have my wrestling partner's leg and I keep pushing for the takedown. He fights back and I push harder. His shoe catches against the edge of the mat. I rock his body over that shoe and his shoe stays put. I hear the bones in his lower leg go, his leg snap, and the bones come out of place.

I feel sick to my stomach as I listen to him screaming. His writhing next to me on the mat as the coaches run over.

Before James disappears, he doesn't pack any bags. Instead, he makes his room look messier. No one suspects him of running.

It's a Thursday night. His stepfather is scheduled to pick him up the next evening to take him home for the weekend.

"You got everything you need?" I ask.

James nods. "Money. I'll throw clothes in a backpack after lights-out."

"Okay, man. Call me from San Francisco?"

James smiles and grabs my hand to shake it. "Oh, hell yeah, Pete."

It's good James is leaving. I've begun to lie to him as well lately. And there's no going back once you start lying to a new friend.

James strokes his weak goatee. The hairs look like the fine white strings inside of a cornhusk. James is always earning demerits for not shaving. He kicks at an old loaf of bread, the mold thick and green inside the bag. "Pete, what're you gonna do about that Ching Chong kid?"

I flex my fists every time I think of Chung Seoul. It's involuntary. James raises his eyebrows.

I exhale. "I don't know, man." There are CDs all over the floor, mixed with the garbage. I pick up an AC/DC album and finger the scratches.

James shakes his head. "Can't fight him again." He bites his lip. "You know that, right?"

Somehow I *do* know that. But I ask, "Why not?"

"Hmm," James laughs. "'Cause you know that kinda kid from juvi, that's why."

I nod.

James says, "Yep, he's the one that can't be beat. Kick his ass again and he'll get some sort of revenge. I can see it in him. He wants something . . . Or lose a fight to him"—James nods twice, licks his teeth—"you'd be his bitch forever . . . and I mean forever."

James knows people. And he's right. There's nothing to say. I try anyway. "I could . . . " But I can't think of a solution.

James pulls at one especially long chin hair. "You know"—the hair sticks out two inches—"you could always kill him."

"Hmm." I nod and think about it.

James kicks a burrito wrapper with his big toe. "It might not be a bad idea, Pete. I mean, you'd make this world a little better."

I set down the CD I've been holding, balance it on top of a crushed Coke can. I mumble, "That's true actually . . . I mean . . . "

James shrugs. "Yeah, he did say he raped those girls back in Los Angeles. And now he wants to rape that new girl. He even told you how he's gonna do it . . . So it ain't like he's a good person or nothing . . . "

I run my hand over my stubbled head, the new nervous tic that I've traded for hamstring stretches. "That's true, man. That's true."

James is gone in the morning.

I walk to Steve's room after breakfast and knock. Steve answers the door looking puffy, tired of being a dorm dean. Supposedly he's been sleeping with a sixteen-year-old sophomore named Vanessa who has a good body but an ugly face. The boys at the school call her a brown bagger. Vanessa and Steve spend two or three hours together most nights. We know that for a fact.

Steve's face is blotchy. He mumbles, "What do you need, Peter?"

"James is really sick."

"Sick?" Steve is still trying to wake up.

"Yeah, throwing up. You don't want to go in there. It smells bad."

"Huh . . . "

I lay it on. "Terrible, in fact. Flu probably. I'll tell his teachers for you, if you want me to."

Steve rubs his face with his hands. He presses his palms against his squinted eyes, then draws his fingers down. "Okay, good. Yeah, thanks, Peter. I'll call the office."

I start to walk away. Then I turn around and come back as James told me to. It's all part of the plan. "Hey, Steve, you don't think I'll get the flu from just walking into his room, do you?"

Steve looks as if the answer is yes but he says, "No. Probably not." Steve is holding his breath when I talk to him.

"Okay. Cool. 'Cause I'd hate to get as sick as James."

"No, it'll be fine." Steve takes a step back and exhales.

"So you want me to check on James at lunch for you then?"

"Yes." He looks truly grateful, relieved, as James predicted. "That'd be great, Peter. Thanks a lot."

"Okay. I'll check on him then."

Later, when Steve asks me if I remembered to check on James, I say, "I forgot. Sorry, man." But James was gone by then anyway.

James is gone almost twenty-four hours before they figure anything out. And knowing James, he's already made it to Missouri.

■

CHAPTER 16

Maria

I start dating Levi's supposed wife-to-be. The girl asks me to prom because I am new and mysterious and bad. I say yes. When Levi finds out, he doesn't drag out his usual phrase about "the Christian thing to do." Instead he looks at me, outraged as a Pharisee.

Fowler and I are good friends now, so I have to lie to him about Mallory. I say, "Mallory and I broke up." We were never dating in the first place, so the breakup is as true as anything else I've ever said about her.

Levi comes into the dorm and marches down to Fowler's room. I can hear his heavy feet and nasal breathing. When he enters the room and sees me, he pushes his glasses up to the top of his nose aggressively. He reminds me of an ill-bred dog.

He cinches his belt underneath his gut and puts his hands on his hips. "Pete?" he asks.

"Yes, Levi?"

"Now, why are you gonna go and do that?"

I sigh. "You mean go to prom, Levi?"

Levi takes off his glasses, crossing his eyes. He cleans each lens and exhales. "No," he says, "I mean go to prom with *my* girl."

I watch him cleaning his glasses. "Last I checked, Levi, she wasn't your girl. She was engaged to somebody else."

But Levi is undaunted. "For now maybe. But she will be my girl. She will be."

"Okay, man. Well, it's only prom. That's all it is. And she asked me. So don't worry too much."

Levi huffs. "Prom . . . "

Fowler and I stand there. I keep opening and closing a Cypress Hill CD case. Fowler says, "You see, Levi, she's been engaged to that Luke guy for the past year, so I'd say you should be mad at *him*, at *that* guy . . . not Pete."

"I'm not mad." Levi scrunches up his face. "I'm not mad. I'm frustrated. You don't seem to understand that I'm thinking about *our* future."

"Yeah . . . " I almost say something mean but then I stop myself. It isn't worth it.

Fowler says, "Yeah, no one means anyone to get hurt, Levi. It's just prom, man. It's just prom."

Levi doesn't look as if he can let it go. But he says, "If it's only prom . . . "

At dinnertime the next night, there's a kid from our dorm doing something in the grass. He's a junior like me, but I don't know him well. He likes to lift weights at night, shoot steroids in his room with the door open.

I watch him bend over and pull up the lid on a water meter hole. I'm curious. "What's in there, man?"

He pats the lid down with the bottom of his shoe. "Nothing."

"Cool." I shrug. "Just wondering." I start to walk towards the dining hall.

"Hey," he calls, "come back."

I turn around.

He points to the ground. "You actually wanna see something good?"

I'm not sure. "Depends what it is."

He reaches down and extracts a wound-up scarf from the bottom of the hole. Huddling close to me, he starts unwinding the scarf. His veins bulge in his forearms at the slightest movements. When he gets to the middle of the bundle, there's a small gun there. It is a derringer over-under .41 pistol. Pearl inlaid in the handle. Blue steel.

The boy puts the gun in my hand.

I hold it as if it is a piece of heavy jewelry. It certainly seems jewel-like, expensive, even though I don't know yet that it is worth ten thousand dollars. "What are you doing with this?"

The boys grins. "It's my stepdaddy's. I stole it."

"But it's a really nice, nice pistol, man." I turn it over, the metal oiled perfectly. "Your stepfather's gonna be pissed."

His eyes flash bright. "I know." He takes the gun back and puts it in the middle of the scarf, rewrapping it carefully. "Do you want it?"

"Want what? The pistol?"

"Yeah, do you want it?"

"Uh . . . " I don't need a gun. But the allure of the pearl-handled derringer is irresistible. I look at the wrapped bundle and say, "Yeah, okay. Sure. I'll take it."

He puts the package in my hands. "Then there you go. I just don't want my stepdaddy to ever get it back."

I nod, feeling the metal weight in my hands. "Okay. Right. Thanks, man."

"No problem." He pats me on the shoulder. Then he walks off toward the dining hall.

I jog back to my room and quickly bury the bundle in the bottom of my sock and underwear drawer. I lay two pairs of boxers over the top of everything. On the way out of my room, I lock my door.

I show Fowler the gun. His roommate, Jamie, comes in and sees it too. Jamie tells a few people. Soon most of the kids in the dorm know I have a gun. But they won't tell. They understand. They would've taken a free gun too. And if I leave my room unlocked, they'll steal it from me the first chance they get.

The gun is useless. To keep it from getting stolen I carry it around tucked in the front of my pants. One Saturday I point it out a car window to scare some college boys from the University of Tennessee who cut us off on the freeway. When we catch up to them, I lean out the window with the gun in my hand. They swerve and jam on their brakes, almost causing a pileup. We take the next off-ramp, laughing so hard that our stomachs cramp.

A few times I take the gun to class. But most of the time it sits wrapped in the scarf in my underwear drawer. After a while, I stop carrying it altogether, thinking kids have forgotten about it. Other rumors become more important.

We have two dorm deans: Steve and Bill. Steve is the ex-navy man, crew-cut and red-faced. He likes to go on runs with the dorm boys. He also enjoys long, one-on-one counseling sessions with girls from the other dorm. But the other dorm dean, Bill, is different. Bill doesn't want to be a teenager. He wants to be a father figure. He is always giving advice and putting his arm around boys' shoulders. A former heavyweight wrestler at Texas Christian University, he is now easily one hundred pounds over his college wrestling weight, big and strong and fat.

One night, Bill catches me as I come out of Fowler's room. Fowler and I have just been discussing which household items will get you high. The common ones: A bottle of Robitussin. Superglue in a paper bag. Chugging NyQuil while taking trucker speed. And a new idea: Vicks aerosol balls if extracted, crushed, and smoked in a bong.

Bill is standing behind the door outside. He whispers, "Come with me."

We walk down the hall to the front of the dorm.

He puts his arm around my shoulders. "What are you thinking, Peter?"

I shrug. "I don't know."

He leans on me. Heavy. "See, you're a smart kid. I can tell. But if you keep going down this road . . . well, it's not going to matter anymore."

I want to say that not a lot matters anymore, but I don't.

He says, "Think about your parents. I met them that one time they came. And they seemed like nice people. Are they nice people?"

"Yeah, they're nice people."

"Okay, then. Think about them. Think about how they'll feel when you get expelled for huffing glue. Huh?"

I nod.

"And you're a wrestler, Peter. You wanna wrestle in college?"

"Yes."

"Okay, then. Let's think about that too. Focus on your athletics. Alright?"

"Alright."

"Get strong."

"Alright."

"Work out a lot."

"Alright." I keep nodding.

"See, there's a lot more out there than getting high. A lot more. But you gotta think ahead. Make choices before you even get in a situation. Decide what you care about. Decide what's important." He squeezes my shoulder with his chubby hand. "Okay. Now go to bed. And don't let me catch you talking about this crap anymore. Got it?"

"Yeah, I got it."

"Good."

"Okay. Thanks, Bill."

"Okay. Good night."

■

Bill and his wife, Maria, live in a one-bedroom apartment at the end of the hall. When Bill is gone one evening, Maria invites me into their apartment. I don't think anything of it since Bill is always so normal and predictable. Fatherly. Kind.

I sit down on the couch opposite Maria. Maria is twenty-five years old and lighter than her husband by 250 pounds. Without him in the room, it is hard to picture them together. She is too pretty for him.

Maria asks me about my family. She asks me about Oregon and about living on the Pacific Ocean.

"I actually never really go to the ocean. It's only an hour away but I don't like it much."

She looks disappointed. "I loved growing up on the ocean. I loved being on the beach in Miami."

"Oh, yeah, that's probably cool," I nod. "Maybe I would've liked the Miami beaches more than the cold, windy Oregon beaches."

She smiles. She stands up and goes to get a Coke for each of us.

While I drink my Coke, Maria tells me about the Cuban culture in Miami. I listen for an hour, then say I have to go do homework.

"Come back tomorrow night?"

"Okay."

When Bill is gone the next night, Maria knocks on my door again. I follow her down the hall, into her apartment, onto her couch.

She gets me a Coke again. We sit on the couch drinking and talking.

"Do you know what San Christo is, Peter?"

I shake my head. "No. I've never heard of it."

"It's voodoo Catholicism." Maria stares straight into my eyes as she says it.

Her stare makes me uncomfortable. "Is San Christo messed up?"

"Yes." Maria doesn't blink. "There's lots of sacrifices. Lots of blood."

I shift in my seat.

Maria continues, "My mother was involved with a priest. She used to take me to the sacrifices when I was a little girl. I remember the blood everywhere . . . " She trails off and looks at me for a long time.

After a minute I want to say that I have to go, but instead I say, "I'm really sorry."

And Maria continues, "Yeah, it was crazy. I remember one night when I was a little girl I had to go to the bathroom. It was dark in the bathroom and I couldn't reach the light switch. I went to go pee in the dark. Then an old woman came in and turned on the light. There was blood everywhere. I hadn't seen it without the light. I didn't know it was there. But I think I could smell it maybe. I was sitting with it all around me. On the walls. On the floor. And there's a smell to it, to blood."

"Uh . . . " I closed my eyes, trying to picture anything other than a little girl in a blood-covered bathroom. I have a memory that never gives up stories and images. I know this story will not leave my brain. I resent her for telling me. I take a huge gulp of Coke so it will burn down my throat. I think about how Coke can eat through a nail. I wonder what a cup of blood would do to a nail.

Maria tells another story about a sacrifice.

I finish my Coke.

When she pauses, I say, "I have to go."

I try to clear my mind as I walk down the hall.

A few nights later, I'm doing push-ups on my cement dorm floor when I hear a soft knock on the door. Maria peeks her head in. "Can I talk to you, Peter?"

"Uh . . . " I stand up. Shirtless, I feel completely naked.

"I really need to talk to you tonight." She looks very upset.

The no I mean to say somehow comes out as "Okay." I grab a T-shirt and put it on.

I follow Maria down the hall. She is barefoot, wearing a red summer dress made of thin nothing. The dress flutters as she walks and I try not to look up her skirt as I follow her. I can clearly see her white silk underwear.

I sit down on her couch again as she locks the door. "Do you want a Coke, Peter?"

"No, thanks. I'm okay."

"Water then?"

"Alright."

She brings us both glasses of water.

She asks how I like living in the dorm.

I say, "It's fine."

She asks about living in Tennessee.

"I guess that's fine too. I miss my family though."

"Yeah." She leans over and touches my hand. "That has to be hard."

I pull my hand back and hold my glass between my two palms, like a little kid, sipping as if the cup is hot.

"Is your mother nice?"

"Yes," I say, "she can be crazy sometimes, but she's a good mother."

Maria smiles. "That's good. I'm glad."

We don't say anything, either of us, for a full minute. We drink water. I look around the room at the pictures on the walls. I notice an old tray table in the corner.

Maria says, "I hope I'll be a good mother too." Her voice cracks.

I say, "Oh, I'm sure you will be." I drink more water.

Maria looks away. "My mother was *not* a good person."

I shift my weight, scooching forward on the couch. I am mad at myself for coming here again. I know better. I say, "Yeah, I remember that. You told me."

Maria leans in. I can smell her shampoo in her wet hair. She says, "My mother used to have me sleep with the priests when I was little. They would come over for dinner and then she would give me to them afterward. They would take me into her bedroom. Lay me down on her bed . . . "

I slide further forward on the couch. I am barely sitting. I look at the lock on the door, a slide bolt. I feel sweat coming out of my pores inside my shirt, sliding down the front of my stomach.

Maria continues. "I think that's what did it. I think that's why I have multiple personality disorder."

I look at her then. I look at her dark eyes and wonder if she's lying to me. I look at her forehead and her face and her cheeks and her lips. I look for a contrived expression. But I find none. She is telling the truth.

"I have at least fifty personalities. Mostly I'm Judy. I'm Judy right now. She knows everything. But I can forget things. Forget things I do . . . I have a map though. Do you want to see my map?"

I want to say no. I want to say no, but instead I say again, "Okay."

Maria pulls out her personality map. It looks like a third grader's rendition of a family tree. The handwriting is all over the poster board, names and traits scrawled at a slant, little faces drawn and colored in.

I wipe the sweat off my forehead with the back of my hand.

Maria explains her personalities. She tells stories of things she's done, bad things, things I don't want to know. She laughs as if she's flipping cards into a hat.

I look at her eyes again, imagining I can see the blood in the small veins there. I try to follow her blood into her brain. I don't know why.

Maria tucks her pretty, dark hair behind her ears. "Judy does the wrong thing sometimes. She does the wrong thing but it's not her fault." Maria opens her legs. I don't notice at first. I don't notice until she puts her hand there. Then I notice.

"I have to go." I stand up.

Maria stands at the same time and hugs me. She clutches me to her chest. I feel her breasts pressing against me. I feel her whole body pressing against me. Her dress is so thin.

"I have to go."

"Thanks for talking to me. I needed to talk to someone. To you. Will you come talk to me again?"

"Uh, yeah. I just have to go now." I push away from her and unlock the door. The bolt slides easier than I thought it would. I throw open the door and step into the hallway. I start to slam the door behind me but Maria catches it. "Thank you, Peter. I really feel like I can talk to you."

"No problem." I turn and walk down the hallway. When I get to my room, I exhale as if blowing away a bad smell.

The next night Bill is gone, Maria knocks on my door at nine o'clock. I pretend not to be there. I lie with my lights turned off, the door locked ahead of time. I hear her try the door. "Peter? Are you there? I just need to talk to you. Are you there?"

I hear her bare feet pad back down the hall.

She comes again the next night. And the next. Then she gives up. She doesn't come again.

■■

CHAPTER 17

The Plan

I slip the gloves on. Wipe the fingertips carefully on the hand-kerchief. No fingerprints. I hold the pistol in my right hand, the knife in my left. I put the gun down. Too loud. I never choose the gun. I only hold it as part of this ritual.

I tuck the handkerchief into my pocket to wipe everything clean afterward. Cleaning and deception.

The instructions for myself, after:

1. Wipe his body. Put on the shoes. Run downstairs and set up. Exit the basement door. Jog to the woods. Get to the stream.
2. Slowly backtrack in my own footprints. Climb the wall with no shoes on, only socks. Let my prints evaporate. Run on top of the wall for three hundred feet. Climb almost to the ground. Put the knife in the ground gap there at the corner and press the clay back into place.
3. Climb up again. Move along the wall. Climb down. Walk backward slowly in soccer cleats like an athlete who is going to practice, like a different person, a person walking at some other time. Wash the shoes carefully when I get back in. Clean the sink meticulously. Wipe everything. Inspect. Reinspect.

4. Go back to my room. Lock my door. Go to sleep.
End of plan.

I open my door by lifting, pushing, and pulling all at once. Noiseless.

I walk down the hall in my bare feet. There can be no blood traces on my shoes when I come back.

I get to the door. Same as the night before. Twenty nights in a row.

I check every night.

I reach out for the handle. Ready. I inhale. Exhale. If it opens, I have to do it quickly: Walk to the bed, put my hand over his mouth, cut his throat, hold him down. Hold him down until he stops fighting.

I picture Chung Seoul's open eyes. I picture his open eyes next to my thumbs. Him biting the heels of my hands.

I push on the door but the door won't give. I push once more to make sure. But nothing. The door is locked. It is locked again.

⊞

CHAPTER 18

The Cemetery

Conflicts often begin with a lie. This one is simple. I say, "Yeah, I dumped Mallory, man."

Fowler says, "That sucks. She seemed cool." But Fowler has never met her. She lives in another state and she was never my girlfriend.

"Yeah," I shrug. "It's fine though."

Fowler looks at me. "Alright then."

The boarding-school world is conducive to gossip. Not only does everyone at my school know that I broke up with my girlfriend, Mallory, but in only two weeks Mallory herself has heard back in New York that I have "dumped her." What I told to one friend in a boys' dorm in Seymour, Tennessee, has traveled to Mallory's girls' dorm, at Woodbridge Prep, New York. In less than two weeks. And I guess Mallory laughed when she first heard the story. Then she got mad.

Mallory is not normal. Her father's sexual abuse combined with her cocaine habit makes her personality sketchy at the edges. She is nervous and unpredictable. And while her unpredictability makes her attractive in a way, she's also scary.

I get the phone call just before ten o'clock at night, just before lights-out.

"Hello?"

"Hello, Peter?"

I don't recognize the voice. I say, "Who is this?"

"It's Tara, Mallory's roommate."

Now I remember. Tara is a bitter, crass girl who's jealous of Mallory.

I say, "Oh . . . okay, right. Tara. How's it going?"

There's a long pause. Then Tara says, "So Mallory's real messed up."

My whole body tenses.

"Are you still there?" Tara asks.

I start nodding my head. I can feel fuzziness in my ears. "What happened?"

Tara clicks her mouth on the other end of the line. "She attempted suicide last night . . . She was upset about you saying you broke up with her."

I lean my head against the cement wall. I can feel my heart punching in my chest, punching like a nail gun. My throat thickens. I open my mouth wide to gather air.

Tara asks again, "Are you still there?"

I say, "Yes." That's all I can say. I can't say anything else.

"Do you even care, Peter?"

I tap my head against the wall. Close my eyes. "What did you say?"

Tara's voice gets deeper. "I said do you even *fucking* care?"

I feel the air compressor surge, shooting a nail through a two-by-six. Suddenly I say, "Fuck you." I don't know why.

"What?" she yells back, "Fuck me? Fuck you, Peter! Fuck you!"

We're both shouting now. "No! Fuck you, Tara! Calling me and telling me *this*? Telling me *like this*? Who *the fuck* are *you*?"

I slam the phone against the cement wall. I slam the phone again and again. I hit it ten or twelve times. Then I drop the phone and step back out of the phone room. A boy is in the hall right then but he ducks inside his room when he sees me coming. I grab a metal garbage can and throw it against the window. The window is Plexiglas, barred on the outside. The garbage can bounces back at me with a loud clank. I kick the can with my shin and yell, "Fuck!"

I run down the stairs and out through the dorm's front door. I run across the commons to the football field, across the field, and up the hill. The hill isn't mowed and the grass is waist-high up there, light colored even in the dark. I run as fast as I can up the steep grass. The grass keeps catching around my ankles, tripping me. I fall down and get up again. Fall a second time. But I keep getting up and keep running.

An old cemetery stands on the summit. I jump the fence there and slow down among the monuments and headstones. I don't read the inscriptions but I drag my hands over the stones as if I am walking the rows blind, counting the dead.

I drop down against the wall of a monument. I start sobbing then, sobbing so hard I think my chest might break, might crack open and spill me onto the stones. I can feel my ribs compressing.

I picture Mallory hooked up to tubes and monitors in a hospital, unconscious in the ICU. I picture the bandages on her wrists, thick and white, covering rows and rows of black stitches.

As I cry into my hands, I picture blood pouring from my own wrists. I move the razor to the already bloodied hand, fingers sliding on the metal, forcing my resolve to cut the second wrist. The razor lies in the sink then, unnecessary, finished. The blood runs down the drain. The blood pinks the running water. The water is so pink now it can't even contain real blood. Mallory keeps pumping the on-water button to hide the sound of her crying. She hasn't made a single noise as she finishes the cutting.

I hear the shouts down the hill. I crawl to the fence. There are flashlights everywhere, around the dorm, the wall, the football field, the gym, the dining hall, the classrooms, and on this hill. Students and faculty. Too many searchers to just be faculty. I can hear one of my soccer teammate's voices on the hill, louder than the rest. He is screaming cuss words in Portuguese.

The searchers can't see me in the cemetery but a group hikes up anyway. I stay low in the shadow of an obelisk-shaped monument. Then someone down at the bottom of the hill begins screaming, screaming as loud as he can. It could be Steve. I can't quite make out what he's yelling. All the searchers pull back, move back down the hill, run back from the far end of the football field, run back from behind the classrooms. All the searchers mass in a large group then quickly file into the dorms. Their search is over.

I watch all this, then go back to the middle of the cemetery.

I think about Mallory again. I think about my lie, how harmless it seemed. The lie was nothing to me. In two weeks I hadn't thought about it once.

But now.

I think about suicide. I think about the shotgun, remember how it tasted in my mouth, the cool air inside its barrel. I remember the smell of the gun oil. I remember the bright yellow flash of the shells, their folded tops, the way their casings fit easily underneath the copper at the ends. I remember the weight of the gun, the heavy stock, the length of the barrel. The lacquer on the wood, the trigger guard, the safety button. The grooved trigger.

I wouldn't taste it now. No. I'm way too angry. I want to hurt someone else. I want to hurt someone else for this. I regret Chung Seoul's locked door. I regret not slitting his throat. I nod to myself. That would've made this better. I picture holding him down for the hundredth time.

But not Mallory. I don't mean her.

I let my mind go.

I picture holding Mallory down and slitting her throat. I start to cry again. I imagine the awkwardness of slitting someone else's wrists, of slitting her wrists. My fingers are sticky and she thrashes weakly. I hold her down one arm at a time.

I lie down flat across a stone grave. I can feel the chiseled epitaphs underneath me like the uneven bed of a river. My body is the water, pressing, changing, beginning to grow stagnant. I feel my blood coagulating in my veins. I am still crying when I fall asleep.

The searchlight wakes me up as it sweeps across the grave markers just above me. I stay low until it passes. Then I look. A sheriff's patrol car. I see another patrol car down on the school road as this car sweeps the hill. The sheriff passes three times and then is gone.

I am cold and numb and do not cry anymore and do not talk to myself and fall asleep and sleep a while and wake up again.

In the morning, I walk back down the hill and go into the dining hall to eat breakfast.

The other kids sit far away from me. People move when they see me sit down within a table of them. I don't see Fowler. I must be late because everyone is moving quickly around me.

After breakfast, a sheriff is waiting outside the dining hall. When I come out, he walks up to me. "Peter Hoffmeister?"

"Yes."

"Could we talk for a moment, young man?"

"Okay." I walk over to his patrol car with him.

He has no sunglasses on. He seems relaxed. He pulls out a notepad. "Are you currently in possession of a pearl-handled derringer pistol?"

"Um . . . " I should say no but I don't care. "Yes, but not on me."

"Right. I'm gonna need that weapon."

"Okay."

We retrieve the gun together. The sheriff and I.

The stepfather doesn't want to press charges against me, so I won't go to jail. But I'll be expelled for possession of a firearm on school property. I go back to my dorm to begin packing.

Steve catches me in the hall. "Can we talk, Peter?"

"Yeah."

"Okay then." Steve motions with his finger. I follow him into his apartment and he shuts the door. "You might want to sit down for this."

I sit down on the edge of the bed.

"So," Steve rubs his hands together. "First, Levi told us that you had the gun. He said that you'd probably shoot somebody. He kept calling you Pete Psycho."

I stay sitting on the side of the bed. I don't have anything to say about that. I never liked Levi, and it doesn't surprise me. What he said to Steve was obvious payback for my taking his "future wife" to prom.

But none of that matters to me.

Steve goes on. "And Mallory called in the middle of the night. She's called probably ten times since."

I'm confused. "What? Mallory called? Is she doing okay then?"

"Hmm. Yeah, that's the thing. Fowler talked to her when she called last night. And I talked to her this morning. Fowler told me I should." Steve stops. He rubs his hands together again as if he's trying to keep warm.

I say, "And what, Steve?"

"Well, you see, girls can be awful mean sometimes when their feelings are hurt. They can do bad things . . . "

"I know, Steve. I get that. But is she okay? Is Mallory gonna be alright?"

"Yes." Steve nods his head. "Yes." He nods some more. "She's gonna be alright. In fact, the thing is, um"—he looks physically uncomfortable as he tries to tell me—"see, the thing is that she was never actually hurt . . . or I mean, well, she was never actually in the hospital or anything. That is . . . she didn't really try to kill herself."

"What?" I say. "What do you mean?"

"Well, Pete, see . . . and this is bad. I know. See, Mallory and Tara decided to tell you that Mallory tried to kill herself. They decided to tell you that, but she didn't actually . . . I mean, it was all a joke. That's the thing. It was all a joke. A joke on you."

I go to my expulsion hearing. The hearing is as professional as everything else at Lion's Gate. There is no student council and no faculty advisory. The board makes no decision. The hearing consists of me and one man, the new headmaster, Mr. Grubb.

Mr. Grubb chuckles as he says that I am expelled. "I never liked you in the first place."

I don't say anything.

"Somehow I always knew you would do something like this."

I take my finals while staying at my soccer coach's house. I'm sure I don't do well on those finals. When my parents call, they inform me that I am going to live with my grandparents in Mountain View, California. That seems odd considering that my parents and grandparents rarely talk. They are not close. But the plane ticket for San Francisco arrives three days after my expulsion.

⊞

CHAPTER 19

My Grandparents' House

They are not what I imagine they'll be. There is a rhythm at my grandparents' house.

We eat nice dinners in the dining room. Then my grandfather tells stories that I've heard since childhood. And I listen.

My grandmother asks me how I feel. "Are you okay, Peter?"

I say, "I'm fine, Grandma. Thank you."

She scrunches her brow and worries. Bad things happened when she was a little girl during the Depression. I am bringing back old feelings, old memories.

I pat her knee. "It'll be okay, Grandma. It'll be okay."

She pats my knee back. She doesn't say anything. She is kind to me.

My grandparents leave me watching late-night TV when they go to bed.

After a while I get up from the couch and snake around in the back of their liquor cabinet. I search for the dustiest bottles in the back row. I know the contents of those bottles won't be missed. Then I stand in my grandparents' dining room and chug until my stomach feels as numb as my brain.

In the mornings I am so hungover that I almost feel angry at myself. I almost feel something.

■

CHAPTER 20

Letterman

My parents let me come home. They don't know what else to do with me. I work at Taco Bell five days a week, closing shift until 1AM I smell like onions all the time.

My baby brother, Ellis, is almost three now. He and I watch *The Little Mermaid* over and over or wrestle on the floor for hours. I teach him how to shoot a double-leg takedown, how to short-arm a front headlock, how to spin toward the ankles on a single. There's a home video from that time period. It is someone's birthday. Ellis and I are in the background wrestling in and out of the frame for half an hour. We quote Disney lines as we grapple and roll through the scene.

In the fall, Coop, his friend Kyle, and I begin attending St. Joseph's Catholic High School. I'm a senior and they're freshmen, but I don't know anyone else, so they're my friends. We sneak out at night to steal beer, then drink it in half-built houses on the Ferry Street side of town. We walk around on particleboard floors, climb on exposed framing, chuck empties through uninstalled windows.

We have a system for beer acquisition. A crowbar and a hammer. Simple and medieval. Cooper chooses them. He carries them around in the cars older boys and girls loan to him. He's only fifteen and doesn't have a license, but he drives himself everywhere.

I wait outside the 7-Eleven with the crowbar resting against the blind side of my pant leg. I can swing it like a short bat from there. I stand at the corner of the store, the back of my head resting against the bricks. I'm supposed to count to ten after Coop and Kyle pass me. Ten seconds will give them enough time to start the car.

Kyle throws open the store's glass door, and Coop cuts through the hole like the high school running back that he is. He has the half rack of Budweiser tucked like a football. He runs low and hard with Kyle sprinting after him yelling, "Go, go, go!"

The 7-Eleven worker comes to the door but doesn't follow.

I count to ten slowly. I want the fight. I want to hit someone with a crowbar.

But when my count is over and no one has chased, I turn and jog the two blocks to Coop's waiting car.

Coop and I play basketball every night. Three hours on the court behind our house. One-on-one. Keeping score. Games to twenty-one.

Coop is a much better shooter than me, but I'm fifteen, two years older and twice as strong. He can't stop my drives. So I go inside for hours. Drive and drive and drive. Or back him down.

I win every game. But he doesn't care. He just keeps playing. He plays as if winning is not important. He plays smooth and cool and positive and keeps popping his jump shot. If I block his shot out of bounds, he just takes the ball back up top and begins again. When I check the ball, he smiles at me.

By the end of the year, every single game is close. Cooper is coming on.

The oak tree grows through the concrete, making it cracked and uneven. The shadows from the tree are thick fingers laid on the ground. We are behind the store, Kyle and I.

The dealer is wearing a Pleasant Hill High School letterman's jacket even though he's about thirty years old. I've never seen him on Thirteenth Street without that jacket. He wears it every day. The shabby white leather sleeves are pocked with grease, mud splatters, and food stains.

I follow Letterman, and Kyle follows me. We need shrooms for ourselves and a bag to sell to a kid named Jonas. Jonas will parcel them off to various freshman girls.

"Through here." Letterman squeezes between the tree and the building. We follow. We are in the alley against the wall, and Letterman reaches inside his coat for the bag.

"Okay," I say. I'm about to pull out my money when two other guys come from our right. One looks like Sasquatch. He is heavyset with brown hair and a beard growing out of the top of his shirt. The other has a biker's black leather jacket on and a Mohawk. If it were a different situation, I would laugh at them. They look like bad TV characters.

The biker is the one who has the knife. I don't see it until it's already out. He turns it twice.

Letterman smiles.

Kyle steps back and bumps against the wall next to me. He weighs 120 pounds. He's a freshman, three years younger than me. I shouldn't have brought him along.

I know I have to accept the deal, whatever it is. I don't even check to see if the bag is light. I know it is. Everyone there knows it is.

I say, "Alright." Pretend. I pull out the roll of cash, trade, and mumble, "Well alright."

"We cool?" Letterman asks.

The guy with the knife flicks his thumb across the blade. It's one of those titanium "cop killers" that everybody carries now if they don't have a gun. He and Letterman glance at each other quickly.

"Yeah, we're cool." I nod. Calm, as if I won't come back and find him later. I don't want him to hide.

"Cool." Letterman shrugs, then drops his shoulders, exposing his throat.

Kyle and I leave the alley the other way. We don't talk as I drive to get Coop. We'll have to borrow a gun.

The cowboy says, "Are we cool?" He smiles with one dead tooth in front. His right hand is extended.

Coop says, "Don't shake his hand, man. Just leave it."

Everyone waits.

But Coop's friend falls for it.

When they shake, the cowboy jerks him forward and punches him with a left cross. The punch knocks him off his feet.

Coop knew all this before. He knew what was going to happen. He'd already choked up on his pool cue. Ready.

When Coop swings, he catches the pool table's light before connecting with the side of the cowboy's head. Green glass sprays like 12-gauge shot across the floor.

I tuck the pistol down the front of my pants, inside my boxers. The metal is cold against my belly. Coop is next to me, and Kyle walks behind us.

"Gonna do it?" Coop sounds hopeful.

"Yep. He *fucking* deserves it."

We walk up and down the street three times. I don't know if we'll find any of them. I start to doubt it. But then we see Letterman outside the Thirteenth Avenue Street Market. He's in the parking lot and he doesn't notice me until I'm twenty feet from him. He steps back into the side of a truck. That stops him. It reminds me of Kyle backing into the wall.

I slot my right hand on the pistol grip. The safety is off and the revolver doesn't need cocking. It is a semiautomatic. I point at Letterman with my other hand. "You fucked up."

"No, no, no, man! It's cool, man! I know it! It's cool!"

"No, you fucked up." I don't care what he says.

He waves his hands wildly, "It's cool, man! Trust me, it's cool!" He is staring at the pistol underneath my shirt. He knows. His eyes get wet at the corners. "It's chill, man! It's chill!"

I can feel the moment coming, rolling down from my head into my shoulder, my arm, my hand. I mumble, "No, you fucked up." I feel it as if I'm about to jump off a bridge into water, do a back flip in the dark. I'm on the railing now, the black water roiling underneath me. I flex and unflex my hand, slide my index finger against the front of the trigger. I remember the cat.

Letterman waves his palms at me. "I got a lot for you! I got everything, my own stash, blues and browns! I got a lot, man! Everything! Just chill, okay? Just chill?"

Coop likes this new development. He steps forward. "What the fuck did you say?" He shoves Letterman in the chest. "What the fuck did you say?"

"Everything, man. I'll give you guys everything." Letterman pats his jacket. There are ounce bags stuffed inside.

Kyle is behind me. He doesn't say anything. Coop is in front of Letterman. Coop is nodding and pointing and smiling as if we've just hit twenty-one in Vegas. He says to me, "Dude, let's take it all. Probably some good stuff here."

Letterman pats his hidden stash again. "Yeah, take it, man. It's real good. Super good. Blue psilocybin. Just chill with the gun." He's still crying a little.

I'm at the edge. I can't stop. I'm on that bridge railing. Hoffmeisters don't quit. "No," I start to raise the gun again. I say to Coop, "Get out of the way."

But Coop holds out his hand. "No. Don't shoot him, man. He fucking deserves it, man, but don't do it. Just let him give us all the drugs. We'll call it good for now. *For now.*" Coop glares at Letterman over his shoulder.

Coop's moral code changes daily. Sometimes revenge, sometimes repayment, sometimes mercy. In this situation, a stolen drug stash is better than a shooting. Coop says again, "Call it good."

Letterman is nodding, bobbing and shaking his sweaty head. "Yeah, man, we'll call it good for now. It'd be cool for now, man. Let's just do that, man."

I remember Cheung Seoul. His face. In my room. I remember planning his murder, what I thought was the perfect, untraceable murder. I remember putting on the gloves, wiping them one last time, walking down the hall toward his room.

I see his face on Letterman's body. I lift the gun.

"No!" Coop pushes my arm down. "No," he says firmly. "Let's take his stuff." He shoves the gun down underneath my shirt.

I look at Coop, confused. He doesn't want me to hurt a worthless, cheating drug dealer on Thirteenth Street, a drug dealer who threatened his brother and his best friend with a knife.

I look at Coop.

Letterman has stopped talking. He doesn't say anything as he glances back and forth between Cooper and me.

Then I see Coop's face as it looked when he was a little boy. I don't know why. I see his bowl haircut and the way he smiled over people's shoulders as he hugged them. I see him as he used to be when he was young, with missing teeth and a smile on his lips.

I relax my hand. I say, "Fine. Fuck it. Whatever. Let's take his stuff."

It is the most willing robbery in history. Letterman practically whistles while he works. He dumps mushrooms into Coop's hands, then Kyle's. Coop tucks his T-shirt into the front of his sagging jeans, stuffing loot down the neckhole.

When we walk away, Letterman is still leaning against the truck. He's mouthing, "It's cool . . . It's cool," as we run across Thirteenth Street in front of traffic.

| CHAPTER 21 |

■

Darkness in the Afternoon

W hile my father completes his neonatal residency at the University
of Washington, our family lives in a rental house six blocks
up from Lake Washington toward Capitol Hill. Even though my father
moonlights as a helicopter-transport doctor, he can't make enough money to
keep us out of debt. So my mother is frugal, our family employing all kinds
of money-saving techniques. We own a Buick that we call The Ick, replete
with roof leaks and moldy carpets, purchased for one dollar from a friend.
We eat spaghetti with red sauce all the time. Rarely with meat. We don't
go to movies. We buy used books at dollar bookstores. And all our furniture
is salvaged from UW campus Dumpsters. Living room chairs are duct-
taped across the seats. Reading lamps are repainted by my mother in bright
colors. Night tables are fitted with unmatched legs. And everything is free.

Cooper and I especially love the game. We jump into the university
Dumpsters as if they were free bins at a baseball card store. We dig and
scavenge and exult in our finds. We come to see the Greek system as a personal charity organization for our family.

When my father finishes school and takes a job in Eugene, we have new
Dumpsters to explore. A fraternity four blocks from our house becomes our
latest hit. Cooper and I check its Dumpsters on the way to play pickup football. We check its Dumpsters each time we stop by the market for candy. We

check its Dumpsters each time we go down to the park. And the fraternity is generous. Soon we're bringing home more treasures than my mother can use.

She finally tells us to stop. We have enough broken chairs in our basement. So Cooper and I begin Dumpster diving for ourselves. We look for decks of cards, broken watches, old baseball hats, outdated copies of Sports Illustrated.

One day, our mother tells us that the fraternity boys are actually out for the summer. "That's why there's such good stuff in the dumpsters right now." She speaks as if she is an authority. "And they're lazy too. Some of them just throw stuff out in the hallway for a janitor to get rid of later. When the doors are open to a fraternity, that means everyone has moved out. Take whatever you want."

Who are we to question our mother? Cooper and I listen as if she's preaching a good sermon.

Cooper and I begin ransacking fraternities on a regular basis. It isn't long before we're going through the rooms, through the dressers, through the closets. Some of the fraternity boys have definitely not moved out. But strangely enough, in four or five trips that summer, we never run into anyone. Not a single person. We rifle through drawers, check under mattresses, and dig through the backs of closets. We find all sorts of interesting things. We know we are stealing. But we are never caught. If a door is open or unlocked, we go in.

I'm a senior in high school. We steal for real now. We steal from cars, houses, fraternities, stores, and other drug dealers. If we can get it without a fight, we'll take it. In case of a fight, we carry knives, hammers, mini crowbars, sometimes guns. Coop and I promise each other that we will never get caught.

"Coop, let's fuck people up instead."

"Yeah, Pete. I love you too," he laughs.

I carve out the front of the plastic honey bear, and my friend Mike puts in the metal bowl. Then he loads the bear with water and ice.

We don't have any weed with us, so I cut and crush my prescription cold medicine with a library card. Then I fill the bowl with tea leaves and this new medicine powder. "You want first?"

"No, go ahead, Pete."

"Okay." I spark and hit it. Black smoke like burning plastic. I can barely suck it in. Then I'm breathing like a sandstorm. Coughing. "Fuck."

The honey bear turns gray.

"This has gotta be terrible for us." Mike crushes more pills.

We smoke the medicine bottle. Get fuzzy.

Hillary writes me a letter from Wheaton College. She says that she admitted that she hated me in front of the entire student body during a ceremony that the school sponsors. And now she doesn't hate me anymore. She's decided to give that up. Even if I took all the family's attention her senior year. Even if I left and made the family look worse than it was. Even if I broke all the rules.

I hold the letter in my hand, wondering what I can write in reply. Then I put it in a drawer next to a rubber-banded stack of a thousand dollars from my latest acid deal.

Mike and I almost get caught stealing pants from a department store one evening. Almost. We have plenty of money, but we'd rather steal. Like Mike says, "It's a department store, you know? Down with the man. Fuck him."

Mike gets tackled by an undercover store security guard in the parking lot. I catch up to them and turn the employee around. He has a tie on. I grab his tie and punch him in the face. Then I throw his head down and knee him hard. His head snaps back and he stumbles, disoriented. I walk toward the car I'm borrowing to get a hammer I left behind the front seat. I'm going to finish this. Then Mike and I will get away.

Halfway there, a security guard punches me from behind. He

hits me on the back of my left ear and I trip forward. My ear puffs out, the cartilage inside torn.

I turn around and start fighting him, then the first security guard jumps back in. I fight them both. I'm swinging at everything.

I fight as if one of us must die. Punch and grapple and gouge and bite.

I yell to Mike, "Run. Get the *fuck* out of here."

I break free and run across the street. Follow Mike.

I'm reading *The Sun Also Rises*. One of my father's favorites.

And I know what's missing for the protagonist. Hemingway's scene in the cab is when I know. I don't understand it physically, but emotionally.

I know.

There is loss like an open pit, waiting in a forest at night. And I understand that.

Girls are attracted to me now, to my strangeness, to my danger, like leaning in too close to a power saw. And I am almost a man. Built like a man. But the girls don't know me, don't know me inside my mind, and they don't really love me.

I drink Olde English malt liquor. Drink HRD vodka. Take trucker speed and Ritalin. Drop acid. I lie awake in the dark listening to the wind rattling the glass.

I try to quiet my mind. Gain control. But I can't.

Instead, I listen to the voice. Count numbers up and down. Hum.

Dark in the afternoon. Clouds thick gray but no rain. Odd midday twilight.

The two men keep walking toward me. They're both so drunk that they're unsteady.

A third man, built like a professional football player, catches my friend Brian at the corner of the yard and reminds me of a grizzly bear catching a newborn fawn. Brian's limbs fling in all directions.

I look over as I continue backing up. I see the football player with his shaved head standing over Brian saying "I'm gonna kill you, you little motherfucker! I'm gonna kill you!" The football player has an American flag tattooed across the side of his throat, the flag rippling and tightening as he screams. His weight easily doubles Brian's, Brian who is only fifteen. Same age as Coop.

I am against a brick wall on the far side now. Brian and the American flag football player to my left. Brian is picked up and dropped on the cement, his body making a weird sound when it hits, like a heavy suitcase landing on grass. Brian doesn't scream. He doesn't make any noise at all.

I'm against the wall and ready to fight the two men in front of me. I'm deciding which one to rush first. The less drunk one. The tougher one. But they're both so drunk it's hard to tell.

The one on the left turns around suddenly and walks away. He says, "I'm gonna go check on the stuff, man."

The other one watches him go, then follows. He mumbles, "Yeah, we should do something about this, huh?" Walks off too.

I stand there for a second against the wall, stationary. It's weird. They just left.

Then I turn toward the fight. Brian makes a sound like a dying bird as he gets punched into the chain-link fence.

I notice for the first time that there's a girl there. Short and blond. I hadn't seen her before. She's standing near the corner of the fence, trying to calm the football player down. She says, "Don't kill him, Todd. Don't kill him. You know you've done bad things too, Todd. You've done bad things too. Remember how you hit that guy with your car, Todd? Remember that?"

The football player isn't listening. He smashes Brian into the fence again. Brian doesn't scream. He's too far gone. His body crumples but the football player catches him before he falls all the way down.

I'm sneaking along the wall now, coming up on the football player from behind.

The girl is talking frantically. "Come on, Todd! You hit him with your car . . . on purpose . . . then beat the shit out of him after. *After.* How's that any better than these guys, Todd? Come on now, Todd! Stop, Todd!"

I don't have anything to hit the football player with. I look for a loose brick or a piece of asphalt on the ground as I sneak up but there isn't anything there.

The football player shakes Brian and I see Brian's eyes roll up into his head. The girl is still talking as the football player raises his enormous right fist to hit Brian again.

And I have to say, "Hey!" I have to stop him. "Why don't you fuck with someone who can fight back?"

The football player drops Brian and turns around. The girl stops talking.

I see the American flag go tight on his neck.

We're in the narrow dog run at the corner of the yard, enclosed by the stairs and the fence, the bushes. I don't see any dogs. Maybe we're the dogs.

The bushes are behind the football player who is thick-necked, tattooed, snorting. He steps toward me, his right fist curled, looking heavy as a five-pound sledge.

I step forward because I have to, because my friend Brian is lying on the ground like a dead person, because Cooper is still inside the warehouse somewhere. I can't run away. So I step forward. But I don't think I can win this fight.

The football player says, "You're gonna die."

And I believe him. I swing at his head.

It all happens in the same two or three seconds.

I punch and miss over his shoulder as he swings and his fist glances off the side of my scalp, barely touching my hair. But that's when Coop's white shirt comes out of the bushes. He's holding something. Short. Coop leaves his feet as if he's jump-serving in a tennis match. Then a sound I've never heard before.

Sudden. The football player's head whips forward. He staggers into me and I catch him as if I'm catching a drunk friend passing out. I catch the football player under the arms with his face cradled into my shoulder. He starts mumbling. He mumbles like a record player on the wrong speed, too slow, half speed, slower, mumbling like a dog growls, like a dog dying, a dog dying in the dog run.

The girl begins screaming but I don't recognize the sound. The sound doesn't make any sense until I see her mouth open, vibrating, and I realize what I'm hearing.

The football player is heavy, so heavy, the heaviest thing I've ever held, and I stand there holding him up, holding up his limp, heavy body. I stand holding him for three or four more seconds because I don't know what else to do.

Then Coop yells at me. "Fucking drop him! Drop him!"

I look at Coop.

He points to the ground. "Fucking drop him, man!"

I say, "Okay," and I drop the football player. I drop him, let him fall, and he falls forward against me. He falls against my knees and I'm still holding him up chest-high, his body leaned against my legs. I push it back, his heavy body, with my hands and my knee and my shin, and he bends awkwardly, bends backward, folding, folding like a broken metal chair, twisted and crumpled. I push his body all the way to the ground. Then I kick him. Hard. I don't know why. I kick him as hard as I can, and I step over him.

The girl is still standing there. Smaller than me. Blond. Screaming.

Coop says, "Come on. Help me." He's picking up Brian. Coop is yelling at all of us, "Run, guys! We have to fucking run, alright? This is taking too long!" Fifteen years old and he's our leader.

Kyle is standing next to the fence with a hammer in his right hand. He looks confused.

I support Brian on one side, and Coop supports him on the other. We get him out into the alley, jogging and dragging his feet.

"Come on, man." Cooper's voice is urgent. He's talking into the side of Brian's face. "Come on, man. We need you to run."

Brain gets his feet under him and tries to jog with us. We still have to support him.

Cooper yells over his shoulder to Kyle, "Are you with us?"

Kyle is right behind us. "Yep," he says. He's still holding the hammer.

We stop after four blocks, at another warehouse, and slide down into the basement window boxes.

We can hear the sirens.

We huddle in the boxes until we're fairly sure the sirens aren't coming in our direction.

I've regained my voice. "Okay, guys. Let's go. Run quick!" I jump out of the crawl space and look both ways.

Coop and Kyle help Brian out.

"We'll go across Seventh as quickly as we can."

We jog, pushing Brian to work his legs. We jog two blocks, then cross Seventh. Four big lanes in the open. It feels like five minutes crossing one street.

Then alleys. Running. Helping Brian. Two parks. Water for Brian at the drinking fountain. More running. We get home and it's almost dark.

Inside, I lock the deadbolt on the front door.

Brian says, "I think I'm gonna be sick, guys."

Kyle helps Brian into the bathroom. Even with the door closed we can hear Brian throwing up. He throws up over and over. Then we hear him coughing and crying. He cries for a long time. His ribs are broken but he's crying about more than that.

Cooper sits down on the couch. I sit down next to him.

I don't say anything.

Kyle sits down in the chair across. He has his face in his hands.

They're all fifteen except for me.

Coop says, "He was killing Brian . . . Fuck . . . He was killing Brian."

We can hear Brian still crying in the bathroom.

Kyle gets up and walks over to the bathroom door. "You okay, man?" He waits. "Brian?"

Brian doesn't say anything.

Cooper says, "Fuck man. I don't know. I hit him so hard."

He's rocking forward and tapping the floor with his shoe. He's holding his head in his hands. Tapping. Every tap hitting the floor like a drumbeat.

| CHAPTER 22 |

■

The Shoulder

My mother buys us four tickets to the Rose Bowl for Christmas. Coop, my father, my father's friend Hirons, and I drive from Eugene to Pasadena in a day, fifteen hours straight, to see Oregon match up with Ki-Jana Carter and the number two Penn State Nittany Lions.

Starting at 4:00 AM, and never stopping for more than ten minutes, we make it to the Motel 6 in Pasadena that evening. We eat Domino's Pizza and sit in our room watching another college bowl game. Then Coop suggests that we play a game of football in the parking lot.

Our game is supposed to be two-hand touch. There are cars, asphalt, sidewalks, and cement curbs, plenty of reasons not to take people to the ground. But then again, my father is playing. He hits Coop hard, pops him, and the momentum takes Coop over the hood of a Honda Civic and down onto the sidewalk. Coop rolls twice before I help him up.

I whisper, "Don't worry. I'll get him. Let's switch."

So Coop and I switch on the next series. I cover my father. He runs a curl and I play back to give him plenty of room to catch a short pass. Then, as he turns, I hit him. Hard. As hard as I can.

I drop my shoulder and forehead and lay into him just above the waist. He flies backward, trips over a curb, and cartwheels head-first into an irrigation ditch.

I don't know that there is a nine-inch cinder block retaining wall in the bottom of the ditch. That's what I don't know.

When my father disappears into the V of the irrigation run, I turn and smile at Coop. Redemption. Then I walk slowly toward the ditch to help my father up, but he's already coming out. He's pushing up with one arm. When he stands, he points at me with that same hand. He can't lift his right arm. It's stuck down at his side, turned in awkwardly like a limb from another animal.

My father's yelling, "Shit! Shit! I knew you would do something like this . . . shit!"

I back up and Hirons jumps between us. "Let's relax, guys! Let's relax!"

My father is still pointing at me. "I knew you would do something like this. I knew it. It was supposed to be two-hand touch!"

"Then what was your hit on Coop, Dad?"

"Coop's *momentum* took him over the car. But I knew *you* would be too physical! I knew it!"

Hirons is between us. "*Both* of you were too rough. Let's just go back inside and take a little time out. Let's see what's wrong with your arm, Charlie."

My father keeps saying "I knew it. I knew it."

Then I snap. "You know what, Dad? Fuck that! Fuck you! You broke my nose on purpose! You broke my nose on purpose and you laughed about it!"

My father keeps shaking his finger at me. He doesn't say anything.

Hirons looks back and forth between us. "Let's just calm down, guys. Let's just calm down."

Coop has retrieved the ball. He's standing there palming the ball against his hip. Watching. He has a look on his face as if he wants to say something, but he doesn't.

We go into the motel room. The room is much smaller than before, and I sit as far from my father as I can. He takes off his shirt and looks at his shoulder in the mirror. The joint sits lower than that of the other shoulder.

Hirons says, "Can you tell what it is?"

My father pushes on it with his left index finger. "No. It's not out of joint but"—he pushes again—"it's soft and swollen there . . . "

"We better get ice on it." Hirons points at Coop. "Can you go get ice from the machine?"

Coop is still staring at our father, still holding the ball on his hip. He nods slowly.

I say, "I'll go with him."

We walk along the outside corridor to the ice machine.

Coop says, "It looks pretty fucked up."

"Yeah, I know."

"But whatever," he shrugs.

I agree with him. "Yeah, whatever."

| CHAPTER 23 |

❖

Expulsion Number Three

I learn a good rule: Don't sell drugs in a mobile home park unless you carry a gun.

They had a hot girl pick me up and drive me here. Then she disappeared.

The house is small and leaning to one side. I count nine guys with thin mustaches. The only three girls at the party are already out of their minds on something I didn't sell them. I have acid baggied in one sock and money rolled in the other. I sell to everybody in the house.

At St. Joseph's, I make a lot of money during the day. But I've begun to sell outside of school. At parties. To strangers.

Someone is messing with the stereo. Pink Floyd's *The Wall* is on. The volume up too high. Someone keeps going back to the part of the album when there's a loud knocking effect. There's a pause and then the whole aluminum house shakes with the knock. Pause. Then knocking again. It sounds like a giant trying to pound his way into the house.

Whatever these guys do normally, it isn't speed. They are way too big. Every male at the party is built like an ironworker. Big boys in dirty wifebeaters. I tell two stories about shooting people just to get off on the right foot. I hope they won't know I'm lying. I hope they think I'm strapped right now.

The acid kicks in. The party devolves. People crawl around the house, psychotic from the black gel tabs. They turn lights off. People I don't know mess with me. The boy with the stereo keeps rewinding and rewinding the knocking. Thirty times. Forty.

A guy in his early twenties sits across from me. He has a baseball hat on sideways. A dirty girl sits on his lap. The guy sneers, "So you sell acid and shit?"

I look right at him. "Yeah."

"So you think that makes you hard?" His face trips blue.

"Hmm." I look at him but ignore him.

"So you think you're hard." He taps his fingers on the girl's thigh. She puts her face into his neck.

I stare at him. We're two dogs. I know better than to look away.

He sniffs loudly. "Motherfuckers always think that."

"Are you calling me a motherfucker?"

He laughs like a tweaker. "Maybe . . . not." The girl pulls her face out of his neck and giggles at me. They laugh at me together.

I don't like to let things go.

But the tweaker says, "I gotta piss." He shoves the girl off of his lap as if she's a cat.

She falls down hard. She giggles at that too, but she says, "What the fuck, man?"

He steps over her and strides to the bathroom.

I get up and leave the house. I start walking toward Eleventh Avenue. I walk down the middle of the road and make cars drive around me. I swerve to block both lanes when cars come. People honk and yell out their windows but nobody stops. I hold my arms out like an airplane.

I go to 7-Eleven and get a fountain drink. Then I walk back to the party. There is nowhere else to go. I don't have a car.

When I get back to the house, everyone is playing tag. They're tackling each other in the kitchen and the living room, knocking over chairs, falling against the couch. Two boys smash against a wall. They are big solid boys and they break the particleboard at the seams. I stand behind the front door with my Big Gulp in my hand.

One of the boys holds his friend's face against the carpet. He rubs his nose in the orange shag as he straddles him. He says, "How do you like that, motherfucker? Huh? Huh, motherfucker?" Then he sits up suddenly and looks manic. He says, "Cat hunting?" as if he's reading an instruction manual. "Cat hunting?" Then he stands up and yells, "Cat hunting!"

The house mobilizes. Everyone scrambles for weapons: A kitchen knife. Two baseball bats. A twenty-inch piece of crooked rebar. An army-surplus machete. A hammer.

"Cat hunting!"

People are running around with their makeshift weapons, shaking knives and rebar in each other's faces, laughing hysterically.

Then they leave. All of them. I watch from behind the door as they scramble out, most of them hitting the doorjamb with a shoulder or knee on the way through. The house shakes with each collision.

I am lucky I am not a cat. I am lucky that they didn't turn on me. I know I am lucky.

I slide out behind the last hunter and leave the house. I can hear the group whooping and killing something behind the next trailer. I walk through the gates to the mobile home park and start home. It's a six-mile walk back to my parents' house in south Eugene, where I have been living for the past four and a half months. I drink my Big Gulp and walk. I walk a long time. When I get home at five in the morning, I'm still tripping hard. I won't come down.

Sunday morning I go to church with my family. The ceiling hazes blue as the pastor preaches. Black smoke hangs like souls in the rafters. I feel sick to my stomach. I only make it through the sermon because I fear getting caught more than I fear the loss of my own mind. My mind hasn't been whole for a long time.

I walk down the hall after the service but I don't enter the youth ministry room. Instead, I slump down against the wall and put my head in my hands.

One of my mother's young friends comes up. She is only a few years older than me. She says, "Are you alright, Pete?"

"No."

She sits down next to me and puts her arm around me. "Do you wanna talk about it?"

I keep my head down. But I talk. I tell much more than I should.

I wash my hands thirty-three times a day and my skin sloughs white, then pink. Cracks open along the crevasses. Blood appears in the cracks, and the cracks turn yellow at the edges. My father has to hide the dish soap. Then the white soap. Bleach. Laundry detergent. Bath foam and degreaser. My father makes a rule: Twice a day. You can wash your hands only twice a day.

I turn thirteen.

Put deodorant on six times each day. And in the seven-step order: on my armpit, armpit, sleeve, sleeve, stomach, back, and one final wipe on the inside of my shirt. When I don't follow the schedule, the bad sweat comes. I smell like a broken animal.

I do two hundred sit-ups before I can allow myself to go to sleep. I have no choice. I count one hundred up and one hundred down. Keep the numbers even:

$$+ 100 - 100 = 0$$

$$10 + 10 + 10 + 10 + 10 + 10 + 10 + 10 + 10 + 10 - 10 - 10 - 10 - 10 - 10 - 10 - 10 - 10 - 10 = 0$$

Perfect.

In advanced algebra class, I memorize pi to the thirteenth digit as it's stapled above the teacher's head. I look up the next one hundred digits and continue memorizing.

I click my teeth and tap my fingers. Counting. I bite my fingernails until they bleed, then I bite them over again to make sure they're all even. They never bleed evenly enough.

There is so much I can't control.

Kyle and I argue with Coop. "We gotta stop all this. We should just ask for rehab."

Coop looks cornered. "Rehab?"

Kyle nods with me.

I say, "That way we don't have to go to fucking St. Joseph's for a while. Everything can mellow out. And we've definitely lost it."

"Lost it?"

Kyle agrees. "Coop, you were high on weed, drunk on OE, tripping on acid, and chain-smoking the other night."

"So?" Coop laughs. "I was having a good time."

I shake my head no. "We've lost it, man. We should get our parents together and tell them we need rehab."

Coop looks back and forth between Kyle and me. "We're *not* saying that we've been selling drugs."

"No, no. We're not. We're just saying that we have a problem. That's all."

Coop points at each of us with his middle finger, the finger he always points with. "And for the record, I think you guys are wrong."

"Okay," I shrug.

"Okay," Kyle agrees.

Coop still points. "This is going to be a world of shit."

Coop is right. That night we admit half-truths to our parents and ask for help. We request rehab over and over. But every parent is too pissed. They offer no help. They want us in trouble, and they send us back to St. Joseph's in the morning as if nothing ever happened.

My mother's friend calls her. The one that I talked to at church. She tells my mother everything I said on Sunday. Within the hour, my parents have called the school and the police.

Father Lopez's index finger is shaking so badly when he comes into my religion class that it looks as if he's having a stroke. He says, "You!"

I grab my backpack. The first police officer rolls up to the curb as Father Lopez and I get to the office.

They go after Kyle first. He looks like the innocent one, a freshman, 120 pounds, thin, and wide-eyed. They press him. They offer him a deal to give me up. I am going to be eighteen in two months. They want to charge me as an adult. But Kyle is loyal.

They put Coop and me in separate rooms where we wait for a couple of hours. The room I'm in is empty, a cleaned-out office. Locked. Coop waits in the conference room. He's in there with all our backpacks and locker material strewn across the table. And Coop isn't one to sit idly. As a police officer interrogates Kyle for two hours, and I sit bored in my locked office, Coop slowly sifts through the pile in front of him. He finds no less than fifteen different notes referencing drugs, drug requests, names, or total profits. And Coop eats the notes. Every last one. He stands in the conference room, working through the pile of incriminating material, eating all the evidence.

The police officer finds only the two hits in a baggie in Kyle's pocket. We'd just sold out our sheet that weekend. There is nothing else on us.

When it's my turn, the officer reads me my Miranda Rights. Then he says, "Do you know what Category 8 Aggravated Drug Offenses are?"

I don't say anything.

"Do you know what delivery of a controlled substance within one thousand feet of school means? Or distribution to minors?"

I don't answer.

"You know you're going to get at least twenty felony counts, right? I'm sure we'll have enough evidence for that. Do you know that you're going to be charged as an adult? You'll be eighteen in less than two months."

I stare at him. Trying not to appear scared.

He looks back at me across the desk. "Do you wanna help yourself out and tell me the whole story?"

I wait.

"Do you know that you're going to go to the Oregon State Penitentiary for the distribution to minors charges? Drug dealers always do for that one. And there'll be other charges too. We know about you."

I stare at him.

"Well, that's how it is. You're young, but you'll still go upstate for a few years. Delivery within one thousand feet of a school is serious business. No judge takes that lightly. And we have this evidence right here to begin with." He plays with the two hits between his fingers. "Kyle got this from you. And he's three years younger than you. That's all we need right there."

I stare at the acid, the evidence in his hand. It is becoming more difficult to stay calm.

"So, do you want to help yourself out?"

I know I shouldn't say anything.

He sits back in his chair, relaxing, letting me know that we'll be in here for a long time. "You know, you'll get softer in prison . . . easier. They'll make you easier." He doesn't smile. It's not a joke. It isn't funny.

Coop and I are sent to stay with the Gobeilles, family friends, a sort of house arrest while awaiting arraignment. Dr. Gobeille's son went to prison, first to MacLaren, then to the Oregon State Penitentiary, so everyone, including the district attorney, figures that Dr. Gobeille will know how to handle us.

Coop and I mostly sit around the house and wait for Mrs. Gobeille to ask us for help with something. We do a lot of yard work. It's supposed to be a hard time but it's pretty easy. I'm with my brother. There's a pool table and a big-screen TV and an expensive, soft bed. I can do thirty years like this.

We are waiting. We are waiting for formal charges and arraignment dates. We hear rumors from friends when we sneak phone calls. No one knows anything real. My father says he has spoken to the DA twice about the case. It's still unclear whether I will be charged as a juvenile or an adult.

I am scared. I don't know what sort of witnesses they have. That is the danger of dealing drugs at a high school. Three-quarters of the school could say something incriminating. And I'm not popular.

Coop shaves my head one night in the upstairs bathroom at the Gobeille's. He shaves my head, then cocks his head back and forth to make sure it is even.

"How's it look, Coop?"

"Good. You look badass with a shaved head. You should keep it."

I nod. "You know I'm fucking scared, right?"

"Yeah, I know. I'm scared for you too, Pete. Worst I'll get is MacLaren, and I can handle MacLaren."

"Yep."

"But OSP?" He grimaces.

I knock some loose hair off. "Fuck that."

Coop palms my head. "Maybe it'll be okay. I ate everything they had on that table. It was a lot of paper. That's a lot of written evidence gone."

"You think they'll have good witnesses though?"

He says, "I don't know," but he nods yes. "There are a lot of punk bitches at that school."

"Yep. That's why I'm scared."

"I know." He doesn't say not to worry. There is a lot to worry about.

∎

Two days later, my father calls. "Pete, I've set up a deal for you. But the deal's your choice. You're almost eighteen."

"Okay, Dad. What is it?"

"Well, it's called Life Challenge. It's a drug rehab and parole program all over the country, started in 1958. We know some people whose son went through it. And it really helped him."

I close my eyes. "So what's the deal then?"

"Well, I talked to the DA, and they're willing to trade all your charges for a successful completion of the Life Challenge program. It's ten months, but it's not prison. And they'll set you up with a job at the end."

I open my eyes. "That sounds pretty good. What's the catch?"

"There is no catch," he pauses, "but since it's minimum security, just a fence and wire and one guardhouse, you can't do the program in Oregon. We're too worried you might leave."

"Okay. So where is it then?"

"Well, we've spoken to the Texas chapters, Dallas and East Texas. You'd be out in East Texas."

"East Texas. Okay. Let me think about it." But I already know I'll take the deal. I am too afraid of a trial not to take it.

"Yep, call me back in an hour. I'll call the DA then."

"Okay." I look around the room. Try to think of something else to say.

My father waits on the other end of the line.

"Thanks, Dad."

"Yep," my father says, and hangs up.

■

CHAPTER 24

Life Challenge

I don't know how my father worked the deal. Ten months in minimum security at the Life Challenge parole and rehabilitation center, East Texas. Ten months in trade for all charges: delivery of a controlled substance within one thousand feet of a school, felony possession, distribution, and distribution to minors. Ten months for all counts as well. I'll have a juvenile, not an adult, record afterward, and I'll be eighteen by the end of the program. So I'll still be able to fully expunge my record.

I have the five-hundred-dollar deposit check in my wallet and forty-four dollars in my sock. I'll move the cash later to keep it with me.

The Dallas Life Challenge representative meets me at my plane. He holds up a sign that reads PETER HOFFMEISTER in black block letters. This is the first choice I have to make. I see him in his shiny blue suit, Suit Man, standing there like a televangelist. I want to walk right past him, but I need the deal. The police officer who arrested me made it very clear what would happen if I went to trial.

So I see Suit Man and stop. I say, "I'm Peter."

He lowers the sign. "Well, okay then."

We drive in Suit Man's Cadillac to the bank. Rush Limbaugh plays loudly on the radio. There is a cold snap in Texas that will last for two weeks, but it's sunny.

At the bank I have another choice. The five-hundred-dollar check is my money, saved from working construction in the summer, and if I want to take the DA's deal, I have to lay down my money. My own money. That's my father's idea. The money is literally a buy-in.

The Cadillac idles in the parking spot. The bank's windows are tinted. Suit Man says, "Do you have your deposit check, Peter?"

It takes me a moment. I already know that Texas isn't right for me. But I can't go to trial. I reach for my wallet. I pull out the check and hand it to him. He says, "Alrighty then. I'll be back in a minute."

At the Life Challenge center in urban Dallas, Suit Man's Cadillac looks to be in imminent danger. I don't know Dallas well enough to be able to name the neighborhood we are in, but I know poverty when I see it. The Cadillac is the newest car on the street by fifteen years, and no building has been constructed or remodeled in the last twenty-five. The sidewalks are junked with huge cracks. A drug addict shuffles past us smelling like infection. I can see the snot running from his nose, glistening against his brown skin. We walk into a building that is layered with decades of graffiti.

Suit Man points upstairs. "This is our Dallas halfway house. You'll sleep here tonight. Tomorrow, I'll take you out to East Texas."

I carry my backpack and suitcase up the stairs. Suit Man doesn't offer to help me. On the eighth floor, we enter the rec hall. There is one dilapidated foosball table, a reading center, three foldout tables, and fifteen chairs. Men are scattered around the room. "Wait in here, Peter. I'll have them start your paperwork before I leave."

"Okay." I sit down and stare straight ahead. All the men are much older than me.

After a while, one comes over to me. He is at least six six. He holds out a hand the size of a dictionary. "Name's Big John."

I shake his hand. "Pete."

He smiles and sits down. I hear the foldout chair squeak and am surprised it holds up. He says, "You gonna do this program?"

"I guess so."

John laughs. "It's better than the pen, kid."

I say, "That's what I figured."

"Figured?" John squints at me. "You mean you haven't been to the pen?"

"To the pen? No," I say before I think about it. I'm usually not honest with strangers. I should have stuck to lying.

John laughs at me. "Oh, shit! Then you don't even know. It's *bad*. See this scar?" He points to his face. "And this one?" He points to his knee. "And this one?" He points at his forearm. "But they can't rape me. Never did."

I say, "Shit," and nod like a little kid. I catch myself. I want to start this conversation over again. This time I'll be harder to impress. I'll say that I've already been to the pen back in Oregon. I'll shrug at his scars.

John goes on. "Probably 'cause I was an O-lineman at Oklahoma State. Can't hold a lineman down long enough." He shrugs. "They put me in the infirmary though . . . a month."

I don't ask anything. I'm already working on the new me: Slow to speak. Slow to care. Unimpressed. This is practice.

John goes on, "Mighta been two months. It was a long time."

I nod casually.

"Gonna get a job next week." John's trying to make me his new best friend. "McDonald's at first, then we'll see." He sits and waits for me to say something. He taps his thumbs together. "You wanna play some foosball, kid?"

The men over at the foosball table are smaller than John but look three times harder. "No," I say, "thanks though. I think I gotta do paperwork."

"Alright." John gets up. "If you need anything . . . "

I learn about the program that night while listening to the other men in my bunkroom. I have the rulebook, a six-page photocopied document, but I haven't read it yet. I've signed both copies, mine and theirs. Signature: *Peter Hoffmeister*. Date: *2/2/95*.

Life Challenge follows Texas State Penitentiary rules, then adds their own on top. No working out, no lifting weights, no running, no push-ups, no pull-ups, no jumping rope, no sit-ups, and no calisthenics. No boxing. No wrestling.

The staff need to be the strongest men in the room.

No TV. No radio. No movies. Only preapproved cassette tapes. Mail is inspected and preread. Mandatory naptime in the early afternoon on weekends. The coffee is decaf. No prescription drugs unless counselor approved. No ibuprofen or Tylenol. Every program member will have a job such as dish duty, garbage detail, etc. Jobs will change on a rotation.

A few specific Life Challenge rules from my allocated rulebook:

RULE #1: I will not smoke.

RULE #2: I will not curse.

RULE #3: I will kick *all* addictions cold turkey.

RULE #4: I will not talk about the past, street life, or drugs or use street language.

My favorites:

RULE #14: I will not go for a walk alone or walk anywhere without staff permission.

RULE #30: I will not murmur or complain.

RULE #35: I will sit erect and attentive at all services, chapel, and classes.

RULE #69: I will not be allowed a visit or phone call until I have been in the program for at least one month.

RULE #70: I will be allowed one phone call per week after at least one month in the center. It will be a collect call and I will limit it to five minutes.

RULE #74: I will arrange my visits for Sunday afternoons and they will include chapel service.

The rule that would become most pertinent to me:

RULE #91: I will accept responsibility and face the consequences for any violation of probation or parole caused by being dismissed or leaving the program.

I am driven to the East Texas center the next morning. Suit Man drives back roads and visits churches and businesses along the way. He shakes hands and chats a long time with different men while I wait in the car. He never explains who anyone is. They all look like the same middle-aged white guy.

While we drive we listen to Rush Limbaugh again. Rush seems to be on the radio twelve hours per day in this part of the country. Rush Limbaugh's laugh makes me want to vomit.

I don't know exactly where we end up. It is a small East Texas town with no welcome sign, dribbling off in the direction of Louisiana. It can't hold more than two hundred people. The Life Challenge center looks like a minimum-security prison added on to a cluster of old gas stations and an abandoned auto shop.

I check in at the gatehouse. They take my tapes, my prescription of naproxen sodium for my sore shoulder, my knife, and my shaving razors. They put those things in a locker and turn the key.

The man in front of me points at my piece of climbing rope. "What is that?"

"It's for jumping rope to stay in shape."

"No. You can't jump rope here."

I don't argue.

He says, "No weights, no running, no push-ups, no sit-ups. Okay?"

I nod. I know I'll do whatever I want later.

I'm in the bathroom stall the next morning. Someone bangs on the wall. "Are you fucking in there?"

"What?"

"Dude, name's Aaron."

"Alright." I don't want to talk to anyone in the bathroom.

"Whatcha in here for?"

I mumble, "Stuff."

"Yeah," Aaron laughs like a crackhead, "me too."

I try to go back to my business.

Aaron bangs on the wall again. "You ever seen the footage of that school bombing?"

"What?"

"The one with the pipe bomb that blew the kid up in the bathroom stall."

"No."

"Well, that was me. I did that."

I flush the toilet. I don't need this guy next to me in the bathroom. But when I come out, he's waiting for me. He keeps talking, as if we already know each other. "Yeah, I only got four years 'cause I was sixteen. Out in three and came here."

"Oh." I try not to sound interested or disinterested.

"Four months here."

"Oh."

"Sucks shit here. But it's better'n prison." He laughs so hard that he leans over on the trash can.

My five cabinmates have gone to prison for rape, assault, assault, murder, and meth distribution. During the first mandatory nap, I keep my eyes wide open.

There is one guy in my counseling group that I like, a forty-four-year-old drug addict who calls weed his "sweet honey." I don't love weed, but that's funny. He makes me laugh. He's dark brown and tall, swaggers like a pimp. When he tells stories, I sit forward and listen. His stories are filled with girlfriends getting cheated on, debts being avoided, violence, lying, and chase scenes. He's always the bad guy. His stories are like good action movies.

The other group members aren't interesting at all. They were betrayed by somebody. It wasn't their fault. It's not fair. Their parole officers are "killing" them. Their wives are "nagging." They like to use the phrase *and then he screwed me over.*

I don't have to talk at first, which I don't mind. I sit erect and listen.

There is only one other teenager in the program, and talking to him on my third day seals it for me. I know I can't do ten months. I don't have a plan yet, but no plan involves ten months in the East Texas Life Challenge program.

I ask, "What're you gonna do when you get out?"

The other seventeen-year-old looks at me. "We don't really get out, man."

"What do you mean?"

"Well, after ten months in here, we still gotta do six months of supervision while we work in Dallas. Then they talk to our POs."

"POs," I repeat. "Work *where?*"

"Work at McDonald's probably. That's where I'm gonna work at least. Most people do. They got some deal or something."

"Six months after?"

"Yep."

"Six more months?"

"Yep."

I do the math. I won't be finished until after I turn nineteen. I start planning to leave.

| CHAPTER 25 |

◨

Hitchhiking

Teenagers fighting teenagers for no reason. High and drunk. Teenagers watching.

We fight for different reasons. Some of us are wrestlers or boxers, others study martial arts. A few study nothing at all. They just don't mind blood.

I agree to stand-up box a Portland Golden Gloves boxer one night, a foolish decision. But I want to know if he's really that good. I get punched maybe three hundred times in our five-minute match and hit him only twice. My eyes swell. My lips swell. I spit and drip blood. He smiles as he breaks his hand punching my forehead over and over. I see him in his cast a week later.

I fight other fights. Fight well on the ground. Grapple. Hook and scrap and get my head in. I like to break fingers, drop an elbow, push my fist into a mouth. I like the feel of teeth turning a head. I can kneel on a throat and finish an opponent, make him tap quick.

There are perennial losers, boys who come to take a beating. Doidge is like that. He never wins but he helps set up the fights. I fight him twice, once at Hayward Field and once in an Albertsons parking lot. He keeps his head down and I underhook him with my left arm. Then I punch him in his kidney with my bare right fist until he drops to his knees and taps

out. He's one of my best friends, and at Hayward Field I hit him twenty
times in the lower back before he goes down. He pees blood after.
  None of us worry about hurting each other. Friends and acquaintances.
So with strangers, it's easy.

After grabbing the knife and the prescription drugs from the
confiscated goods cabinet in the Life Challenge gatehouse, I say,
"Don't try to stop me. You got that?"

The gatekeeper nods quickly. He is short and fat and sitting in
a chair where I put him. He is sitting like a grade-schooler. He
starts to turn the chair around.

"If you move . . . "

He stops. He says, "Relax, man. It's a voluntary parole program. You can leave. I only have to call the sheriff's office."

"You can call after. Got it? You can call *after* I leave."

"Yeah, okay. After." He puts his hands up.

I run out of the gatehouse door onto the hard-packed East Texas
dirt. My backpack isn't heavy, but it's heavier than I would've
liked considering that I have to run two or three miles. It's a half
mile just to the first turn, open ground that won't hide a jack-
rabbit, much less a person.

Every second, I expect them to drive up on me. I only have a
one- or two-minute lead on the call to the sheriff's office. I dodge
through three alleys in the ghost town, hide behind a phone booth
and wait, but I don't see anything.

Life Challenge is a drug-rehab parole program, minimum security, and I don't know what law I might have broken by leaving.
I don't even know what kind of legal requirement I have to be
there. I know there is some deal with the DA in Eugene, but no
one has explained the deal to me. So in leaving, I'm not sure how
quickly the authorities will be notified. Or if they'll even care. Of
course, I just threatened my way past the gatekeeper and took a
knife, so I know I'll have to watch out for a sheriff's patrol as long
as I'm near here.

At the edge of town, a Mexican family gives me a ride in the back of their pickup. They speak no English, but they keep smiling through the cab window at me and signing thumbs up. The woman has a baby on her lap who is sucking on its fingers and reminds me of my baby sister Maddie back in Eugene.

The family drives me forty miles away from the Louisiana border, toward Dallas.

When I get out I say, "*Gracias. Muchas gracias.*"

They both smile, crinkling their eyes at my poor accent.

I stick out my thumb again in whatever town this is. A few cars pass. I walk for five minutes. Then a car pulls over behind me and I turn to see that it's a patrol car. Black and white. A police officer stands up out of the driver's side. "Can you step over to the vehicle, sir?"

"Uh, yeah. Okay." I walk toward the patrol car, pulling down my sweatshirt over my jeans to hide the knife.

The police officer goes around the back of his car. "Do you know where you're going this evening?"

"Yes," I say. "Dallas." The truth is that I've only planned on going west.

The police officer's hands are empty and open, hanging like a gunslinger's. I notice that his pistol strap is unsnapped. He has on Oakley Blade sunglasses and stands to my side. "Do you have a driver's license and five dollars on you?"

"What?"

"A license and five dollars." He hooks one of his thumbs on his utility belt.

"Yeah, I do . . . " I slide off my pack and reach into my top zipper pocket.

The police officer explains. "Here in Texas, five dollars and a license proves that you're not homeless."

The criteria seem arbitrary. "Oh." I show him a five-dollar bill and hand over my license.

"Lemme just go run this." He steps back around to the driver's side of the patrol car.

Again, I wonder how quickly the sheriff's department was notified of my departure from Life Challenge. And I wonder how quickly that sort of information gets out to a scanner, or if it even gets out to a scanner at all.

I wait five minutes. The radio crackles. The police officer mumbles into his CB. I listen hard while pretending not to.

It's five o'clock. The sun is on a quick trajectory, dropping like an arrow shot over the ocean. It was warm earlier, but now I feel the cold coming.

The police officer walks back around the car. His face doesn't show anything, his eyes still hidden.

"Oregon?" he asks.

"Yeah."

He has my license in his hand. He doesn't offer it back. "So what're you doing in Texas?"

"I'm traveling." I try to make my voice sound low and calm.

The officer turns his head and looks up the street at something. "Okay then . . . and are you hoping to end up in Dallas? I mean . . . is that your final destination?"

"No, I'm going back to Oregon." I actually haven't gotten that far with my plans yet, but I need to say something.

"Leaving straight away?"

I wish he'd give my license back and take off his sunglasses. I'm beginning to feel claustrophobic. "I'm going back as quickly as I can." I can hear my own voice losing its confidence.

He nods slowly. "Hop in then. I'll give you a ride." He holds my license out to me.

I take it. "You're going to give me a ride?" I try to sound grateful, but I'm not. As the car pulls away from the curb, I wonder where we're going.

I notice the fat around the officer's jaw. The Oakleys cut lines into his cheeks.

We drive out into the flatlands on I-20, empty forests of white birch. The sun is down to the horizon now, and it's getting cold outside, cold even for January. I know it might freeze, and I become grateful for the ride. The car rolls along smoothly and the heater pipes warm air through the car.

We don't talk much. I watch the road ease by, relax my shoulders and neck. My backpack is between my knees, jammed into the space there. I loosen my lower leg muscles and wish I could stretch my hamstrings.

When we pull over on the shoulder, I'm confused. There isn't anything there. No town. No houses. I look at the police officer. "What's up?"

He smiles, his sunglasses still on. "County line. This is as far as I can go."

I look around. It's almost dark. The birch stick up like bleached bones. We're twenty miles past the last town. "Here?" I'm beginning to understand. "Here?" I point at the forest.

"Yep. You gotta get out here."

When I open the door, the cold air rushes in like water filling a sinking ship. I step out and drag my backpack after me.

The officer smiles again. His Oakleys still pinch. He leans over to my side of the car, his elbow touching the passenger seat. "Hitchhiking in Texas is illegal. You take care now."

I mumble, "Thank you." I don't even know why.

The officer nods his head, and his sunglasses don't wiggle. Then he shuts the passenger-side door and drives away. He drives forward, right across what he called the county line, and I follow his rear lights for at least a mile until I am sure that he has lied to me. As if I didn't already know.

I look around. There is trash scattered across the shoulder of the road and down into the ditch. Twenty feet from the road the birch trees begin. "Fuck," I say aloud. It's cold. I say "fuck" again.

I try to hitchhike. It doesn't work. My shoulder gets tired from holding my arm out. I switch arms, walk backward. Then it is dark. The cars rush past me like meteors, bright headlights merging to form a shower.

I stop. Walk down through the ditch to the edge of the woods. I lean against a tree and pee, trying to think of something to do. I consider building a debris shelter, a pile, but the leaves from the fall are old, thin and rotten on the ground, not enough to cover me and hold any sort of warmth. I zip my pants back up and stand at the edge of the forest. I can't think of anything better to do than walk along the road.

When I return to the highway and put my thumb up again, I don't actually hope for a ride. I don't hope for anything. I hold my thumb up because holding my thumb up feels like a choice.

I walk forward as I have walked the last two miles. My backpack has been rubbing unevenly, pulling to the left, and I consider stopping to repack. But I don't. I just keep walking.

The night drops down into the low thirties. Near freezing. I can feel the temperature up my cotton sleeves. I can see it on my breath. I remember the night in Maine a year before, when I was sixteen.

Ben and I threw a rod on an inland interstate, and the Jeep was totaled by the time I fought it over to the side of the road. It was late November, ten o'clock at night. Negative five degrees. We pulled blankets and a down coat out of the back hatch, tossed the gear down into the ditch next to the road. We played rock-paper-scissors to see who would hitchhike and who would stay with the Jeep. I lost. I had to stay with the Jeep.

Ben got a ride with the first trucker that passed. We were lucky. It was five minutes before another vehicle passed. And most people drove that strip of Maine at one hundred miles per hour.

The temperature continued to drop. I stood in the ditch next to the Jeep, waiting as if Ben might return at any moment. Then I realized how long he'd probably be gone, how long I'd have to wait for him. Two hours, maybe three. We were a long way from the next big town.

I had the down jacket on but I was not warm. I did a hundred jumping jacks, then jogged back and forth over a little twenty-foot course. I was warmer after that and lay down in the grass, covering my legs with three blankets. I pulled a fourth blanket

over my shoulders and wrapped it around my face. It was negative ten now, maybe colder, and I tried to cocoon myself. The
jumping jacks, the running, and the blankets worked, and I was
warm enough to fall asleep.

A big truck woke me up, blasting its horn as it went by. My
face was down in one of the blankets. My neck twisted. Whole
body twisted. I was too cold now. I tried to stand up and couldn't.
I dropped back and curled up again. Buried my face.

Time. Huddled. Rocking and shivering.

Then a flashlight shined through the blanket. "Pete, you okay?
Pete?"

I opened my eyes. Ben was standing above me. A man in a
down parka next to him, arms crossed. "Shit!" he said. "That boy
looks cold."

"You okay, Pete?" Ben pulled me to my feet.

"Uh-uh." I tried to get up but couldn't stand or walk straight.
My back was too cold to straighten all the way.

Ben had his arm underneath my shoulder. "Let's get you in the
truck next to the heater."

The Texas freeway is nowhere near as cold as that night in Maine.
So I know I'm fine. On I-20, it's five degrees above freezing, and
the shivering stays away as long as I keep walking. I know I can
trudge forward all night. I know I can. And I resolve to do just
that when the Cadillac pulls over in front of me.

The Cadillac is long and smooth, a restored 1974 with immacu-
late green paint. The automatic window is already down. "Wanna
ride?" The driver is a middle-aged man with pallid skin, thinning
hair, and expensive clothes.

"Sure. Thanks." I get in, relieved.

"Name's Daniel."

We shake hands. "I'm Pete."

"Nice to meet you, Pete." Daniel's blinker flicks, and we accel-
erate onto the freeway in a smooth roll.

Man's greatest invention: the car heater. I settle back into my leather bucket seat. Even with my backpack at my feet, there is plenty of room.

The car is decadent, lavish, with an oiled dashboard and leather recliners, clean ceiling cover, and tinted windows. Even the eight-track and radio are original and pristine. The speakers sound too good.

Daniel is tuned to a seventies rock station. "Stairway to Heaven" comes on. Even though my mother always said this song is evil, I like it. I close my eyes and rest. Everything is too good.

"You like cigars, Peter?"

"Cigars?" I open my eyes.

"Do you like Cubans?" Daniel points to the dash compartment in front of me.

"What?" I say.

"I keep cigars in there."

"And you want me to open it?"

He nods. "Yes. If you want one, get out two."

I open the compartment and see the battery-operated humidor clipped to the wooden box. There are seven cigars inside. "Are you sure?"

Daniel smiles. "I don't mind at all, Peter."

I hand him the first cigar and he mouths it to seal the tobacco wrap with saliva. I do the same with mine. We use the car's push-in lighter to light the cigars.

I puff a few big clouds and smell the good, Cuban smoke. "Stairway to Heaven" finishes. I am warm and relaxed and content. I try to think of the last time I was this happy. Certainly not in Texas, not since being expelled, not since being arrested. Not at my last high school, St. Joseph's. Not at home.

I search my brain.

Then I have it. The Rose Bowl. Coop and I had tickets on the opposite side of the stadium from Hirons and my father. We stayed at the car and kept throwing and catching and laughing with each other after they left to find their seats. Then we locked the car and walked along the outside of the Rose Bowl, joking around, sharing a forty of Olde English that Coop had smuggled in his bag. It was sunny and warm for the start of January, the light coming cleanly through the tree branches. My midmorning buzz made everything fuzzy at the edges. I put my arm over Coop's shoulders, and he smiled at me as he used to when he was a little kid. We were in a crowd of one hundred thousand people, and I was happy just to be there with my little brother.

I think about the Rose Bowl as I sit in the perfect Cadillac. I think about Coop as I smoke a Cuban cigar while hitchhiking in a restored car across Texas on a January night.

Then Daniel says, "So, where are you going?"

"Dallas tonight. I guess . . . "

"Oh, okay."

We both puff at our cigars quietly. I like the smell of the interior of the car. Smoke and leather. The slight engine smell of the heater.

I ask, "Did you fix this car up yourself?"

Daniel smiles. "I had it done piece by piece. But I take care of all the little things."

I nod approvingly. "It looks really good."

"Thank you, Peter."

Daniel likes to say my name. I notice the idiosyncrasy but it doesn't bother me. He can say it as many times as he wants as long as I have a warm ride.

Daniel ashes carefully in the tray. I do the same.

"Do you have family in Dallas, Peter?"

I exhale. "No. In Oregon. I'm going back there."

He nods.

"Hotel California" is on the radio now. I like Zeppelin better.

"So, you're going to stay a night in Dallas?"

"Yeah."

He puffs twice on his cigar. "Where are you staying?"

I look at him and shrug.

"Oh." He doesn't say anything else. We smoke. "Hotel California" gives way to Pink Floyd's "Brain Damage," good music. A Doors song follows. I hate the Doors. They remind me of carnival music.

As the Doors wind down, I realize I haven't asked Daniel much of anything. And I don't want to be rude. So I ask, "What do you do?"

"Do?" he smiles. "I'm a lawyer, Peter."

"Oh, okay. Cool."

"Are you interested in the law?"

I shake my head. "No. My mother always says I could be a lawyer because I like to memorize baseball statistics. But I don't think so."

"You don't want to be a lawyer?"

"No. I mean, not really."

Daniel ashes his cigar again. I lean forward and ash mine. There is a rhythm to our actions: Smoke, talk, ash. Smoke, talk, ash. I like the rhythm. The rhythm feels like good counting.

"So, what do you want to do, Peter?"

I puff twice, hold the smoke in my mouth, then exhale slowly. The smoke slithers up my jawline like gray snakes. I watch it ease past my eyes. "Maybe be a writer?"

"You like to write?"

"Yeah, definitely."

Daniel points to the road in front of us. "Well, traveling is a good start . . . and trying new things."

"Yeah, I guess that's true."

We pass a sign that reads DALLAS 16

I pull my water bottle out of the side pocket of my pack and take a drink, careful not to jostle my cigar, careful not to ash on the seat. "You want some water, Daniel?"

Daniel waves me off. "No, thank you, Peter."

The car is rolling at seventy. Smooth and dark and clean. My cigar smells perfect again, after the water, and I realize that the cigar will only be half finished when this ride is over, and I will be able to smoke it as I walk around, as I find a soup kitchen or a teen shelter. I think of how good it will feel to smoke out in the open air, while walking on the sidewalk in the cold. A cigar can make a person feel rich. Happy.

I think of earlier that day, in the bunkhouse, watching my bunkmate sleep, watching a rapist snore through his congested nose, and I smile at how much my situation has improved.

I don't even care about the police officer anymore. I think of being dumped on the side of the road, twenty miles out of town, and it doesn't matter now. I am riding in a nice car. I am smoking a Cuban cigar while talking to a kind, middle-aged lawyer. I am listening to classic rock on quality speakers.

The radio DJ chooses Pink Floyd again, "On the Turning Away." I remember when I was first given this song by an older girl in math class sophomore year, how she passed the cassette tape to me as though she was passing me drugs. Up her sleeve until I took her hand. I listened to that tape twenty times before I gave it back to her.

I am singing along to myself in my own head when Daniel asks me the question. And his tone implies that the question is a normal question, a question anyone might ask a stranger at a bus stop. But it isn't normal. Not from a stranger. Not from a man three times my age. With an exhale, he asks, "Have you ever had a homosexual experience, Peter?"

I don't hear him correctly. I am still thinking about the song and the cassette tape and the math class and the older girl. "Huh?"

"Have you ever had an experience with a man?"

The way he says the word *man* isn't good. *Man* means him. *Man* means Daniel.

I look at him. He is grinning as if we are still talking about being lawyers or writers, talking about where we live or where I am headed.

"No," I say quickly, hoping the topic will go away.

"Mmhmm." Daniel puffs on his cigar and I don't like the way he does it. I don't want to smoke with him anymore. I can't sit in this car and smoke with him anymore. I put my cigar out in the ashtray, smashing the lit end with more force than necessary. The cigar stub wobbles in the tray like a severed finger.

A road sign reads DALLAS 12.

Twelve miles. We are already passing through suburbia. We'll be in the city in a few minutes, and I will be out of the car, walking on the street.

"It's going to be cold tonight, Peter."

"Yeah." I don't look at him. I don't want to give him too much prompting now.

"Do you want me to get us a hotel room for tonight, just so you're not cold?"

I look at him hard, the way I looked at my cabinmate the rapist. Daniel is still smoking casually. I can see the wrinkles at the corners of his mouth, the beginnings of old age.

"No." I say again. "No, I don't."

We drive a mile. I stare out the window at the yellowed freeway night.

"Peter, I know good things to do."

"No," I say. I spit the word as if it is flat and sharp, a small piece of metal. Then I add, "I told you, *no*," for emphasis. Be clear.

Daniel nods.

We drive another mile. The city isn't coming fast enough. I look over at the speedometer and notice it is only tacked at fifty-five now. Daniel has slowed down.

There's a smell in the car, tangible, the smell of unwanted words coming. My brain hums. I know he is going to push it. I put my hand in my pocket. I feel my knife.

"You could just lie there, Peter, and I'll make you feel good. I'll . . ."

"Shut the *fuck* up! And *stop* saying my name!"

Daniel holds his right hand up. "Easy, okay. Don't worry. I thought you just might want to know how good it feels to be with a man."

"Fuck you!" I look at him, still unbelieving. He is relaxed. Smiling. I can see the fillings on the sides of his molars. "I'm warning you."

I am finished with this. Nothing else today. Nobody else today.

I am finished. I grip the knife, feel the smooth handle in my right hand, across my body from Daniel.

A sign says DALLAS 6.

Another mile passes. Five miles to go.

"If you just lied there, I'd . . . "

"Let me out of the car, you perverted fuck!" I don't say what I'll do if he doesn't. I don't say anything about that. I know though.

Daniel doesn't slow down. He keeps the Cadillac at fifty-five. He doesn't pull to the shoulder.

We pass an off-ramp. I can feel my heartbeat rise, my breathing, my adrenaline. He didn't stop. He isn't going to stop. He isn't going to let me out.

He doesn't know that I am finished with him. "Take the next off-ramp, *Daniel!*"

He keeps driving. I don't know why he is still driving that car, why his foot is still heavy on that petal. I clench my fist around my knife handle and look at Daniel.

He is smiling, still smiling. He bobs his head again. "I can be *really* gentle, Peter. I think you need someone who can . . . "

"Take the next fucking off-ramp, you fucking piece of shit!"

I clench my fist on the knife. I unbuckle and turn toward him. I picture swinging the knife like a hay hook, stabbing and pulling.

Daniel's face is still smiling as if he isn't human, as if I'm not human, as if none of this is real, as if I haven't told him three times to stop the car.

I feel as if I am watching my own life, as if the car and the man and the knife and the boy are no longer real, just action, just plotline. And I know the ending already. I will take his car. I will drive all night. I will dump his body somewhere so remote that it won't be found until it has been picked clean by every scavenging animal on earth.

Daniel is still smiling.

I see his jawbone. That bone will be clean, bleached by the sun, white, as white as any bone I have ever collected for my mother's bone sculpting.

My hand is on the knife and my heart is turned sideways. Pump and speed. All my emotion is cornered fear.

The hum comes into my ears. I close my eyes. Feel the hum encouraging me.

I envision Daniel's throat stabbed until it gurgles. Gurgling and the hum. Picture ripping his body across the seat and taking the wheel. I am listening to him die in the passenger seat as I drive the Cadillac. I can hear the sucking sound in his throat. His trachea torn open.

Daniel doesn't slow down. I see a car on an off-ramp a half mile up. See the car's taillights and its deceleration. Wait for the feeling of our own car slowing down.

Nothing. The Cadillac is pinned at fifty-five, Daniel's shoe heavy.

I tell myself it will be nothing. It will be nothing. I don't want to kill him. But some creatures must die. Rationalize. Death is natural, cyclical, important for balance. I ready myself. Do it quickly. Do it quickly. Do it quickly.

I will hit him once. Puncture once. Then grab the wheel.

Be accurate.

We are going fifty-five.

The off-ramp is there now, up, to our right.

The humming throbs in my temples.

My knife hand is so tight that I don't know if I can swing my arm. I force myself to relax. Be accurate. Breathe. Puncture cleanly. Be accurate. Do it under the next overpass, in the shadow.

I am relaxing my shoulder as the car swings wildly onto the ramp, over the divider with a bump.

We decelerate.

I am still clutching the knife in my tight fist when Daniel pulls into a gas station at the T of the off-ramp.

He says, "I'll be right back." Goes into the store.

I sit in the passenger seat. Then I stuff the knife back into my pocket, open my door, get out, and pull my backpack from the car like dragging a man's body.

I fix the length of a strap without thinking about it. I am having trouble returning to my own mind.

I shoulder the pack.

"Here, Peter."

I turn around.

Daniel is standing there holding something out to me. "It's a map, Peter. I bought it for you."

"Oh." I say.

Beneath the bright shine of the fluorescent lights above, Daniel is already dead. He holds the map. He says, "Take it so you know where to go."

I keep staring at his face, trying to imagine him alive. The hum is dissipating.

I take the map. Then I say, "Thanks." I don't know why. I'm a Hoffmeister. I can't change.

"Sure. You take care, Peter."

Daniel walks around to his side of the car and gets back in. He reverses the car quickly, pops it into drive, then rolls away.

I take off my pack and open the main compartment. I shove the map to the bottom of my pack like an ugly family secret.

▦

CHAPTER 26

Dallas

T hirteen. I jump off a small cliff at the Oregon coast and tear a tendon on the bottom of my right foot, heel to toe pad. I'll be on crutches all summer, wear a series of casts until December.

My mother keeps asking me to go to the pool. "You could dangle your other leg in the water. Or you could read and suntan."

I shake my head. "No, thank you. I'll stay here alone."

I watch a baseball game each day, either the ESPN pick or the Braves on TBS. When there's no baseball on, I sit up in my room doing push-ups or pull-ups or reading. Alone in my room, the voice returns to me. I hear the humming first, the machine's drone, the consistency of the pistons. Then the voice. It is insistent but calm.

Adjust that picture on the wall.

I obey. I am used to obedience. Conditioned to the obedience, conditioned to the rhythm of our interactions. Command, obey. Command, obey. Command, obey.

Fold back the cover on your bed.

I hop over on my good leg to complete the task.

Put the baseball bat in the corner.

I use the bat as a crutch until I get to the corner, then hop back to the *middle of the room and kneel down. I kneel with my butt on the heel of my cast. I wait for the next command.*

Move the dresser.

I know it means the oak piece of furniture, six feet tall and as heavy as I am. I hesitate.

Again.

Move the dresser.

The voice doesn't get louder. The voice speaks in the same insistent monotone no matter how many times it has to repeat a demand. The uniformity is unsettling.

I mumble, "I can't." I explain to the voice. Hum with the hum. Hum the same pitch. The machine closes around me like wind gusts in a heavy storm. I become deaf. I exhale hard to rush my own ears. And when the rush comes I close my eyes.

Move the dresser.

The voice is so clear. I have never disobeyed before, not once in five years. Disobedience is not an option.

I look at my cast. Stand up on my good leg like a broken heron.

I hop on my left leg until I can lean against the side of the oak dresser. Then I use my body weight and push. Nothing.

The voice watches me. Waiting.

I push harder, tensing my whole body. The dresser moves half an inch out of its indents in the carpet. I strain again. The dresser yields another half inch.

The voice wants me to move the dresser in front of the door, to block the door, three feet further. Somehow I know this, know all the voice's desires.

I continue to gain half an inch at a time. Sweat breaks out on my forehead, then my back.

The voice waits for me to finish my task. It waits like a man in the dark outside a lit window.

I move the dresser the last half inch, to the doorknob, just touching. Then I collapse on the floor, panting. I want to throw up. My arms are outstretched like a cross.

The voice speaks again.

Move the dresser back.

I stare up at the slope of the white ceiling. I blink my eyes, feeling the sting of the sweat running off my forehead into my eyes and ears. I don't stand up. I don't get to my knees. I don't obey.

The hum continues. The drone increases and my head becomes a beehive. The voice stays the same. Always.

Move the dresser back.

Four gunshots. A car stripped to its frame. Two meth heads weaving double helixes on the sidewalk. I walk into the 7-Eleven and buy ninety-nine-cent Little Gem doughnuts. There's bullet-proof glass for the counter boy. Dirty windows. Outside, a teen-ager the same age as me walks up. Snot connecting a loop from his nose to his mouth. I give him a doughnut. He leaves, mumbling, "Fucking soup kitchen and shit."

Speeding cars. A domestic fight. Automatic gunfire, close. I duck down but I don't hear the bullets hit. I crawl into a hedge in front of a paint warehouse, dig a hole in the leaves, pour my backpack's contents out. My white underwear looks funny on top of the pile of brown leaves. I wiggle my head and shoulders into the backpack so the cold air can't bite my face. I pull blindly at the leaves and clothes, piling them over my legs. I go to sleep.

I wake up cold. I know I have to move. The neighborhood is quiet now. I look at my watch. It's 3:17 AM I repack my bag with stiff hands. I pull both sides of the hood of my sweatshirt in and hold them tight with my teeth. I begin to walk.

I walk four or five miles to the bridge across the river. There isn't much river left, just three dry channels and a dirty trickle, but the bridge spans a quarter of a mile. I walk across. The sun starts to come up. I see the green of the grass on the hillside underneath and I hop the railing and slide down toward one of the cement pylons. The sun touches the grass and banks off the pylon. It's twenty degrees warmer in that corner, so I lie down and fall asleep. The sun puffs up from the southeast. I begin to sweat, warm and comfortable, and my hands uncurl. I slip off my hood and go back to sleep.

Somebody nudges me awake with his boot. A cop.

I squint up at him. He's outlined like an angel in the sunlight.

He barks, "Do you have five dollars and a valid driver's license?"

I try to wake up. "One minute." I hold up a finger. "I'll grab 'em."

I find the license in my top pocket. Five dollars in my sock. I hand them over.

"Seventeen years old?"

"Yes."

"From Oregon?"

"Yes."

He studies the picture on the license, then looks at my face. He goes back and forth. "You can't sleep down here. This is city property."

"Oh. Okay."

He waits for me to get up, so I do. Stiff, but much warmer than the night before, I shoulder my backpack. The cop follows me up to the topside of the bridge.

"Don't go back down there."

"Okay."

"Okay then." He nods. Then walks away.

I am downtown. Gray buildings and traffic. Business people in nice clothes. I look for a mission but only find the Greyhound station, which is good enough.

I rest.

The first day in the bus station. A big man crashes through the door, falling forward like a car on an icy road. He balls up awkwardly on the floor. The security guard stands him up and throws him out.

I nap in a chair.

A transvestite in a blue-sequined dress talks to me about missing his sister.

People leave for Tulsa on the 11:25 bus.

The O. J. trial is on TV.

The bus for Oklahoma City is delayed until 12:05 PM

I write a letter to a friend from school.

Three little kids argue while their father watches TV and picks his nose with his thumb.

El Paso is right on time at 3:30.

I eat seven packets of free saltines, drinking them down at the water fountain.

It gets dark outside.

The security guards kick out all nonticketed passengers. Only passengers are allowed to stay inside at night.

I wander around as the temperature goes below freezing again. A homeless veteran named Red Man shows me the air vents. The vents blow seventy-degree air all night long, and Red Man says he likes Dallas. "It ain't one of them fucked-up cities where they keep the homeless off the vents by pumping scary noises and shit through the tunnels. Ain't no man can sleep to that, mother-fucker."

We sit down on a vent together. It is nicely warm beneath me. Red Man falls right to sleep.

I don't sleep. After a while, I get up and walk down the block.

I smoke a joint in an alley with a kid named Arnold. He tells stories that are all lies. My lies are all true. He gives me a joint for the road, literally.

The next day, I sleep in the Greyhound station, under the counter, near the phones. They ring sometimes. Not too often. Mostly people use the phones to call and ask for money. One man above me cries through a whole conversation. I look up at the bottom of his wet beard.

Two teenagers get in a fight. One wears a gold chain around his neck that doesn't break even when he gets hit in the throat. He says, "*Tu madre, puto,*" and spits on the ground. A security guard shoves him in the chest. The security guard looks bored.

I go down by the train tracks that night. Red Man is there again. He asks me to ride with him. He says railyard bulls never bother him. He says, "They gotta let the immigrants immigrate." Then he brags about twelve social security cards and unemployment, trading food stamps for weed. He says, "I got more weed than God."

I tell him that I'll smoke or eat anything.

We smoke a couple joints together. He asks me to travel with him again, but I tell him to go on without me. I don't need to hop trains yet. I still hope I can get a friend in Eugene to send me money. I'll use the phone in the bus station tomorrow. I'll be one of those callers. I've seen them cry. I know how to do it.

I wander into the new downtown at daylight, into the business district again, brokers and bankers chucking hellos before they enter through revolving doors. The glass and steel lobbies remind me of sterile pet store aisles.

McDonald's downtown looks familiar, orange and brown and plastic, so I go in and buy two hamburgers for ninety-eight cents. They taste like artificial home flavoring, same as back in Eugene. I promise myself two hamburgers per day. Forty-one days of food money left in my sock. Forty-one days of McDonald's. I know that forty is a holy number. The flood. The Jews in exile. Jesus in the desert. What is forty plus one? Is that good or bad for me?

I return to the bus station with food in my stomach. Nap. Eat more saltines.

O. J. Simpson on television again. Pictures of Nicole. She was pretty before he stabbed her.

There is a college kid next to me with pre-worn-out clothing and a pristine Yankees hat. I picture every Yankee fan I never liked.

Bus to Shreveport departing late. Last call.

A spider crawls across the floor, a spider as big as a little kid's hand.

There is coffee that tastes as if it was made from instant crystals. But it's free. It's the best coffee I have ever had in my entire life.

There are no more saltines in the condiment tray.

I write two more letters in my notebook. I don't tear them out to send. I write a to-do list:

Get money sent here.

—Eat saltines before they run out each day. Not too many.
Don't get caught.

—Budget one dollar per day for other food.

—Travel back to Eugene.

—Find new place to live.

—Finish high school.

I collect-call Doidge but get his mother. Then I call Mike's house and only get the answering machine. I go and lie underneath a counter. I count wads of gum stuck to the Formica above me. Thirty-seven.

Last call for the bus to Little Rock.

I go to sleep.

When I wake up, I make another collect call to Doidge, and this time I get him.

"Hello?"

"Hello, Doidge. This is Pete."

"No way! Fuck, Pete. Fuck!"

I say, "Yeah, I know. I know," over and over.

Doidge promises to raise money at school. He says, "I'll call it the Bring Pete Hoffmeister Home Fund. I'll collect money in a big applesauce can. Get it in the hallway and shit. You'll see. I'll get you all the money quick. Give me three or four days. A week, tops."

I can't help smiling. Doidge cracks me up. "Thanks, man. Thank you so much. I really appreciate it."

I hang up the phone like ending a prayer. Go back to sleep underneath the counter again.

When it gets dark outside, a security guard kicks me in the shoulder to wake me up. I stand and rub the knot. He kicked me much harder than he needed to. When I look at his face, it looks as if he's going to laugh.

■

Outside, the air tastes like loss. Half awake now, I can feel the rhythm of my blood pumping into my brain. I'm just out of REM, sleepy mouthed, and there's a girl outside who's beautiful and Latina with crooked teeth and a hopeful bag under her arm. The bag says that she's outside to get fresh air, and air only, because she has a ticket in the pocket of her tight jeans. The jeans have two razorblade slits like deposit boxes. I wonder if she cut them herself.

The girl says, "Hi." She scoots over next to me against the wall. "Are you going north?"

"No. Maybe west in a few days, a week or two, but I don't know. My friend might send me money Western Union."

"Oh," she touches her bottom lip. "I'm going to New York to model."

"Cool."

She says, "My friend's boyfriend hooked me up with an agent that took a bunch of pictures of me to put in my portfolio." She smiles. Her teeth overlap perfectly.

I look at her face. She's younger than me. More naïve. I hope she's really going to New York because I can tell that she wants that to be true more than anything.

"Are those your pictures?"

She's already holding them out as if she knew I was going to ask. Or she wanted me to ask. And that's not good. She's standing here outside a bus station in downtown Dallas, Texas, with her portfolio in her hands, asking strangers to look at her modeling pictures.

"Wanna look?"

"Okay." I flip open the binder. But by the second page I see that this girl is even younger and prettier and more innocent and more vulnerable than I thought, and none of the pictures in the book have her wearing much of anything at all. There are five straight pages of lingerie shots. She's wearing lace of every color and sometimes she's on her knees or sucking on a finger and the whole thing is almost pornographic and I feel even sadder than I did before.

I flip quickly through the last pages and say, "Your pictures are great." That's what I say, "great."

She says, "Thanks," and smiles as if she's off to her first day at kindergarten.

"Be careful in New York."

She says, "Oh, I will. I always am," and manufactures an expression on her face that is only younger and weaker and more like a new wet rabbit than anything I've seen yet. So I have to get away from her. I have to get the fuck away from this naïve girl before I see any more.

"Yeah, I have to go," I say. "I have to meet this guy."

She looks at me confused, but she says, "Bye."

Later, I wander down by the bars. There are drunks coming out everywhere and it's late and this skinny guy in a silk shirt bumps into me and I push him and he laughs at me and I keep walking.

Then a big, greasy white man stumbles up to me and puts his hands on my shoulders. He says, "Hey man," as if he knows me, and I don't shove him off of me right away because I can tell he's the kind of guy who might bite my face. He's wearing a stained wifebeater and has blotchy skin and shoulders that are big and strong and round and fat and sprouting hair like bug antennas.

He says, "Are you Aryan?"

"What?"

"Are you Aryan?"

I don't answer. I try to shrug him off and leave.

He says, "My wife likes Aryans. You could come home with me if you want to." He still has his hands on my shoulders.

I push his hands off carefully, slowly, not wanting a man as big and drunk as him to get all mixed up. But he's already mixed up and he begins ranting about how his wife would like to do all sorts of things with a kid like me. He says, "She loves strong Aryan kids like you and she likes it up the ass." He says, "I'll just sit in a chair in the room and watch from a corner. We do that kind of stuff all the time."

I can smell his breath, and his breath is fishy and drunk and rotten. It flows over my face like a sour tide.

My brain is humming now, and I can hear the clicking. Clicking and sliding. I see the man in his own apartment, in a corner, with puke all over the front of his shirt, yellow now instead of white, and there are streaks of brown bile where he ran out of stomach contents from the puking. He's in a fetal position and he looks up at me like an animal that's been shot, and his eyes are bloodshot from the puking and the bleeding.

I blink and he's taller than me again. In front of me. He pushes me with two hands. He tells me, "Come fuck my wife up the ass."

I can feel the humming and humming. Loud voltage growling in my brain. Like the deep-throat growling of a big dog. And doors slamming everywhere. Wooden doors, car doors, metal doors, the doors of my old school, my old house, my grandparents' house. I wrap my fingers through the chain link fence of the Life Challenge compound. I feel the iron rusting in my palms. There's black at the corners of my eyes, everything closing in.

He pushes me again. "Come fuck her, you Aryan fuck!"

My brain is not my brain anymore. I say, "I'll come and fucking kill you. That's what I'll do. I'll fucking kill you right here."

He says, "Fuck you," and laughs as he backs away.

I have my knife again, and there's blood on it that's not there yet, and I can smell the blood that's rivering through the man's arteries and veins, and the blood smells to me like an iron skillet that's been heating too long. Warping. Making a pinging noise.

I know that I've lost something now because this keeps happening, and I feel as if this is all I ever come to, to this place, this knife, this feeling, almost killing, and I wonder that I'm not drunk because I feel fucked up and cold and hot, and this man, the drunk man, he's backing away from me toward a parked car and he trips over the parking meter and stumbles and takes a few steps and there's a wall he can follow along and he's scuttling back into the doorway of the bar and his off-white shirt gets hazy like cottonwood down floating off the river back home but it's hot in the spring there, back home, when the cottonwoods are dropping, and nothing about this night is even warm at all except my fist around the handle of the knife that's still cold, and there's the smell of the river water, the water in the air, and water everywhere, over my eyes and the city and the night, and I wonder why the water's not frozen because it's cold, cold every night here, so fucking cold, and no amount of weed will warm me up because I'm a long way from home and my bed and my room and my house and my family and anything and everything and everyone that I have ever loved, and I can sleep on a dirty floor with gum and spiders and garbage and wrappers and ants and dust and spit and cum, and I can sleep here and wake up, and I can sleep here and wake up again, but no amount of sleeping and waking will ever make it right.

◼◼

CHAPTER 27

A New Day

I wake up in the Greyhound station and my mind is quiet. Better. I've slept all morning underneath the counter. Four hours. I am warm and relaxed and remember the night like drawing a picture with my eyes closed. Formless and unclear at the edges. The model girl and the drunk begging me to go home and fuck his wife. But I'm okay now. Past noon on a new day. And the new day comes again.

The television sets are on. More O. J. Simpson. I check the condiment trays and find six packs of saltines. I take three. Eat slowly. Walk back and forth to the drinking fountain. I can't see a security guard anywhere.

I sit down and write another letter to a friend. Write one to Mike. Write one to Doidge. Write one to Coop. I leave my letters in my journal and know I'll never send them. But I write as if I will. I ask questions in the letters, asking how school's going and if they're hanging out with any new girls.

I go back to sleep with my head and arms draped over my back-pack. Two more hours. Wake up at four o'clock and walk down to

McDonald's again. I pull a dollar out of my sock and order hamburgers. Eat and read the newspaper. Drink three cups of water. Use the bathroom. Go back to my seat in a booth.

Everything starts over.

◼

CHAPTER 28

Home

The Bring Pete Hoffmeister Home Fund works. Doidge gets $60 from my old track coach Mike Yeoman, then collects the rest of the $180 in the halls. Sends me the money the next day.

I ride three and half days home: Texas, New Mexico, Arizona, California, Oregon. Sleep upright. Write in my journal. Trade stories with a kid from Oklahoma. Hold a single mother's baby. Smoke weed outside of Wilcox, Arizona. Laugh with a group of men who joke in Spanish slang.

It's midnight in Eugene as the bus comes down Pearl Street. I'll go to Mike's house first and ask his mom if I can stay there. Reenroll at South Eugene High School in the morning. Five classes spring term, and I'll have enough credits to graduate.

A box of childhood photos thrown out across the kitchen table. Cooper with his arm draped over my shoulders before scoring four touchdowns in his first high school football game. Cooper as a little boy crying when the family rooster died. Cooper with his sawed-off .177 pellet gun, "Squirrel Killer," laughing like a car accident.

The second night home, I call my parents from the Dari Mart payphone.

My mother picks up. "Hello?"

"Hi, Mom."

"Oh, Peter . . . " she starts to cry.

I wait. Control my voice. I know what I have to say, and I practiced saying it as I walked down to the store.

There must have been sign language on the other end because my dad joins us on the line. "Peter?"

"Yep." I try to sound cold and distant, invulnerable.

"Where are you?"

"Eugene. I'm back."

"Oh my God . . . " My mother exhales, relieved.

"But I'm not coming home. And you two can't make me. I'm going to live with Mike and Pris this spring, go back to South. Got it?"

My mother's really crying now. "Oh, Peter, we don't care about the details anymore."

"That's right, Pete." My father sounds as if he's crying too. "We're just glad that you're safe. That you're back in Eugene. Not in Texas."

"Yeah, well, I am safe *now*. I'm fine. And I'm almost eighteen. So I'm just going to live with Pris. Okay?"

"Yes, Peter."

"Okay, Pete."

Now this is the part I've practiced. "So maybe we'll talk sometime down the road but not now. I don't want to talk now. I don't want to see you. I don't want to get *fucked* with or *sent* anywhere. Got it? I want you two to leave me alone. Alright?"

There's a pause. Then my father says, "Alright, Pete. We're just glad you're safe. We're glad you're home."

My mother says, "And we love you, Peter."

I want to say "I love you" back. But I say, "Okay. Good. Well, that's it. I have to go now."

▪▪

CHAPTER 29

Life of the Painted Bird

I enroll at South Eugene High School because I know it has no ties to my previous school. No information on me. And Lane County hasn't set up a consequence yet for my skipping out on the Life Challenge program. The detectives don't even know that I'm back in town.

My English teacher's name is Mrs. Stahlberg. She holds me after class one day until the rest of the students are gone. She says, "Can I take you to coffee after school?"

At first I think she's hitting on me. But she's middle-aged, has only one breast from surviving cancer, and taps on the wood she places in her bra.

I think about it for a moment. "Okay. I'll meet you there."

When I get to the coffee shop after school, she's already waiting. She's bought us each a coffee. She points to my cup. "I didn't doctor it up because I didn't know how you take it."

"Oh, yeah, thanks. I guess I drink it black." I've never had anything but cheap, bus-station coffee before, coffee that had to be drowned in sugar and cream. But this coffee actually smells good.

"I wanted to meet you here because you're a reader. I can tell that by how you talk in class. Do you read a lot?"

I nod. "Usually . . . at least I always did as a kid."

"So I have these for you." She pulls out a stack of used books tied together with a ribbon. "A present." She slides the stack across the table.

"Whoa, thank you." I untie the ribbon, start reading titles and looking at the covers. The first book is *Siddhartha* by Hesse. I read the back.

Mrs. Stahlberg says, "It's about a young man's journey. Spiritual and metaphorical. You might like it."

"Thank you." I turn the book over twice, then pick up the next one: *The Painted Bird* by Jerzy Kosinski.

"That's a journey too, but different. It's a harsh story. You know what I mean?"

I look at her and smile. "Yeah, I think I know what you mean."

We drink coffee and discuss each book she's giving me. She explains conflicts and characters. She gets excited and spit gathers at the corners of her mouth as she tells me stories about the authors.

When I leave, she hugs me good-bye, which doesn't feel strange. I thank her again.

That night, I light two candles next to my bed in my new room and read until late. I read half of *Siddhartha*. I read the rest of *Siddhartha* and all of *The Painted Bird* over the next few days.

In class, Mrs. Stahlberg asks for my opinions when we discuss themes. She asks me to explain metaphors and allusions and to detail rhyme schemes. She brings me into every discussion.

One day, she pulls me up in front of the class and has the other students interview me. She says, "Ask him where he's been during high school."

They ask, and I talk a little bit about moving around. They ask why I moved so much, and I say, "I got into some trouble."

Twenty students raise their hands.

After class, Mrs. Stahlberg holds out two movie tickets. "These are for you."

"What?"

"Movie tickets."

Again, I think she's asking me for a date. But she's not.

She says, "Take somebody with the other ticket. It's an interesting film. I think you'll like it."

I take the tickets and go with Mike.

A week later, I skip English class. I feel terrible.

Mrs. Stahlberg sees me in the hall at the end of the day. "I missed you today."

"Yeah, I skipped."

She laughs. "I like that honesty. What are you reading right now?"

"Shakespeare." I think she's asking about my classwork.

"No, no. On your own."

"Oh, *Sula*. By Morrison."

"And do you like it?"

"Yeah. It's intense. Incredible writing."

Mrs. Stahlberg puts her hand on my shoulder. "I'm so glad you're reading good writing."

That afternoon, I get my letter from Lane County. The letter I've worried about.

The detectives counted on the written evidence they'd collected, but Cooper had eaten every note that day in the conference room at school. The detectives never interviewed witnesses, so now all they have is two counts of LSD possession. That's it.

The letter from Lane County specifies my penalty: one day at Skipworth juvenile detention center, six months of mandatory urinalysis screenings at White Bird Clinic, and six months of mandatory drug counseling with a county counselor. Cooper, Kyle, and I are all charged as minors, our records to be expunged six months after our eighteenth birthdays.

I go to Skipworth on the appointed day. Pee in front of a county worker. Start counseling the next week.

| CHAPTER 30 |

■

Gun Incidents

I'm living at Mike's house on Kincaid Street in Eugene, renting an upstairs room for one hundred dollars a month. Cheap. Pris, Mike's mother, loves me like her own son. She says, "I want you to finish high school and grow up into a man."

Next door, a bored fourteen-year-old boy lies on the grass in his backyard and throws little rocks over the fence at the windows of my room. I can hear the rocks pinging as I read, pinging against Pris's window.

I get up and slide it open. Yell, "You better fucking stop that."

I close the window and wait for the rocks to hit again. I sit with my book but don't read.

I hear another ping and jump up. Someone is swinging in the tree behind the house, in the alley. I grab my BB gun. From the window, I shoot into the alley, into the apple tree covered in thick, green leaves and bright blossoms. Because I can't see well, I shoot at bits of clothing and shaking motions in the branches. I don't know that I've shot the wrong kid, the wrong neighbor, a ten-year-old, until I see him drop out of the tree. The little kid is screaming, holding his grade-school face in his grade-school hands.

I close the window and whisper, "Shit." Slide the BB gun under my bed. Sit down on the floor. I pray that I didn't shoot a BB into the child's eye. I think about a year earlier, at Woodbridge Prep, when I made a similar decision.

In the evening, I walk around the block and knock on the back neighbor's door. A white woman answers. The woman looks unkempt and angry. She wears hippy clothes that belong at the Saturday Market or the Country Fair. She is the biggest marijuana dealer on this side of town, but I don't know that yet. She says, "Come into the kitchen."

I enter the house, hoping to apologize, and follow the woman to a table in the kitchen. There is a black man seated across the table. The black man says, "Sit down, young man." The man's voice is resonant, like a black man's voice in a movie, like a famous black man preacher. I wonder if he *is* a preacher.

I sit down in the chair that the preacher points to.

The preacher looks across the table a long time before he speaks. Then he says, "Do you realize what an issue this is, young man?"

"Um, yes, sir. I want to apologize profusely. What I did was absolutely wrong. Absolutely wrong. I'm very sorry."

"But do you understand what an issue this is?" The preacher points a thick index finger at me.

"Yes, sir. I mean, I think so. I am *very, very* sorry."

"No. Do you understand what an issue it is that *you,*" he pauses, "a *white* man," another pause, "shot a *black* child?"

I clear my throat but don't say anything. Until this moment, I didn't know that the child was black. The child had not appeared black when he was hidden in the leaves. The child had not appeared black when he dropped out of the tree holding his face.

I scan my brain for any information I might have missed. I remember that the child had dark hair. That was true. But the child's skin was light, very light, lighter than my own. Looking across the table, I don't think that it is genetically possible for a child so light skinned to be the son of this dark man in front of me. It's all very confusing. But I know that weird things happen, and recessive genes can be strong. And besides, I didn't even mean to shoot that boy. I meant to shoot a different neighbor, the rock thrower, the teenager, nearer to my age, a kid with blond hair. And even *that* is not important right now. I'm here to apologize. So I stop my convoluted thinking and say, "Um, yes sir. I understand. And as his father, you must be extremely . . . "

"I am not the child's father." The preacher speaks as if he is dropping a large rock on the table.

The situation cannot get worse. I apologize three more times.

A month passes. It is a warm day in early June. The neighborhood kids are having a water fight on the lawn in front of the Kincaid house. I'm with Mike and his little brother in the front yard, playing with the neighborhood children. We have squirt guns and a hose. Everyone is laughing.

A group of children mob me. I wrestle them, break free, and hose them down. The kids remind me of my own brothers and sisters. They are laughing as they jump back on top of me. More wrestling.

Then a five-year-old boy hits his own sister in the face. The little boy is small but wiry, and the hit is a loud slap with his wet hand. Everyone stops playing.

Everyone looks at the little boy. He is embarrassed. He might have done it by accident. He hesitates. Then he points at me. He points at me and says, "He slapped my sister."

I smile. "No, I didn't. It's okay though. Just tell the truth."

The little boy gains strength from his own lie. "I *am* telling the truth. *You* slapped my sister." He points his index finger that is smaller than a flesh-colored Crayola crayon.

The sister is crying and holding her cheek. She looks around at the faces of everyone there. She doesn't know the truth. She is unsure. Then she runs away, runs toward home, around the block, to the house directly behind the room that I rent from Pris.

And I realize which house she is running to.

I don't go apologize this night. First of all, the apology would be a lie. I didn't hit the girl. Second, the apology would be futile. No one would believe my apologies a second time.

So I move out. Move out of Pris's house. Mike and I were going to move out soon anyway, but the little boy's lie pushes me out early. I pack my one backpack and small suitcase. That is all I need. I own fewer than one hundred items. I've counted.

When I go to leave, Pris gets up from the chair where she's been reading and chain-smoking. "I love you, Peter."

I've got my backpack on and my suitcase in my hand.

I hug her with one arm. "I love you too, Pris."

It's summer now and I'm using the payphone at the minimart near my complex. I have no phone in my apartment. I'm in the phone booth when one of my old high school track teammates shows up, driving his father's Lexus. The teammate's name is Jonah, and Jonah's great tragedy in life is that he was born white. He's been attempting to remedy that tragedy his whole teenage existence by talking in a way that he thinks sounds black, as if skin color is determined by word choice and inflection. By affiliations.

I smile when he see him. Jonah is silly. I know that saggy pants and rapper slang do not an African American make.

But Jonah's always been cool to me, so I greet him. "What's up, Jonah? How are you?"

Jonah does not return my smile. Instead he glares at me. "Yo, you's hella wrong, hella wrong, B!" Jonah's waving his hands as if there are bees swarming in front of his face.

"Huh?" I hang up the phone. I think I heard him wrong. "What?"

"Yo, I hear what you done, son. I hear." Jonah nods like a bobblehead. "I hear about it, kid."

"What? What are you talking about?"

"Yo, what you did is hella wack. You think you can jist slap a little black girl like it's nothin', son? You think that?"

I'm not amused by Jonah anymore. "Whoa, whoa, Jonah! Chill out! Relax. Get the fucking facts straight. Now what you heard isn't actually true. It's not true at all. So you better not spread that rumor around."

"Rumor? It ain't no rumor, kid! I know who told me, and she's straight." Jonah pulls his pants up in the front and sniffs for emphasis.

I begin to walk toward him. "Now I didn't hit that girl, man. Her brother did, the five-year-old. He hit her and then he didn't want to get in trouble for it. So he said I did it."

"Na, na, kid. Na, na, na . . . "

"I didn't hit her, Jonah . . . " I'm getting frustrated. "But I'll hit you. You better shut the fuck up."

Jonah says, "I should jist . . . " and clenches his fist, but he's backing around his father's expensive car as he speaks, opening the car door.

I continue walking toward the curb. "I'm telling you, you should just shut the fuck up, Jonah, and not talk about stuff you don't know anything about."

Jonah starts the car and pulls fifty feet away for safety. Then he opens his door again and yells back. "We're gonna find you, son! We're gonna find you!"

I hold up both of my hands. Point to myself. "You found me right now, Jonah. Come get me. Come get some!"

Jonah shakes his head. Still leaning out of the car, he yells, "We're gonna find you, son, and we're gonna gat you!" He makes a pistol motion with his left hand.

I'm still pointing to myself. "Come gat me now then, mother-fucker! You're here now, huh? Gat me now!"

"No, we'll find you, B. We'll find you." Jonah ducks back into his father's Lexus and drives away.

I come out of my apartment a few nights later to go to a party. I have only a hooded sweatshirt and twenty dollars in my pocket.

Nothing else. There's a man smoking by himself down the apartment row. The man is smoking and holding something in his other hand. The bottom porch lights are all smashed out and it is dark where the man's standing. I'm walking toward him when I realize what he's holding. I know for sure when I hear the slide of the action.

There's an alley to my left, across the open gravel, and I cut hard. I run through the alley, down a block, across a street, and into another alley. I hide in a hedge until I'm sure no one is following me.

I don't go to the party. Don't go home. I stay out all night.

I'm sitting in my apartment reading a book the next day, sitting with a sawed-off shotgun across my knees. I wait with my shotgun for a knock on the door. I wait and read a book, tap the gun's modified stock, the sanded pistol grip, touch the trigger with my index finger.

I spend weeks inside my apartment that summer, reading, waiting, holding a loaded gun in my lap.

■

CHAPTER 31

The Lord Giveth

W e meet at Allann Bros. Coffee early afternoon on a Saturday. She's late, and I think she might not come.

When she walks in, she looks older than I remember. Smaller. More fragile. Like a paper cutout of an early-middle-aged woman.

She smiles and her eyes crinkle at the corners. I walk over and hug her. I feel six inches taller.

She hugs me for a long time.

"Hi, Mom." Her hair smells the same as always.

"Oh, Peter . . . "

We get coffees and sit down at a table.

She has her hands on her journal, a mosaic of magazine shards glued to the cover. She never leaves anything as is.

We both sip our coffees.

She looks up. "How have you been?"

"Good, Mom." I have two hands on my coffee cup. Protecting myself.

I say, "I've been reading a lot. Some good stuff." That's true. I have been reading a lot, for both comfort and pleasure. At the moment, Anaïs Nin.

My mother opens her journal. She's going to write down a book title if I give her one.

So I tell her about *The Painted Bird*. "It's a survival story."

She writes it down.

"But I don't know if you'd like it." I tap my cup. "It's pretty harsh."

"Oh, well . . . " She puts her right hand up in the air, waving it around lightly. She doesn't say anything more.

We drink our coffees for a while. Smile at each other.

"Have you been painting, Mom?"

She's sketching now on the paper in front of her. An outline of my head. She looks up in flashes. "Yes." She draws my hair. "Alice Neel stuff . . . or I hope."

"That's good. Really good." I look around the room at the bad art in the coffee shop. I say, "Alice Neel's pretty amazing."

My mother nods, then shakes her head, "I'm not disciplined though. I don't have a set painting time or anything, but I need one. I need to be disciplined. You know what I'm saying?"

I nod. Take a drink of my coffee. "Yeah, that's hard. Discipline isn't easy."

My mother has forgotten her coffee. She's adding lines to her sketch, building my jawbone, the new facial hair I'm growing. A goatee. She says, "You know that night in Tennessee?"

I ask, "Which one?" but I know exactly which one.

"The one when you ran off. After that girl lied to you. That girl Mallory."

I bite my lip. "Yeah. I know which one you're talking about."

"Did you know they called us that night?"

I shake my head. "Called you when?"

She sketches my neck. Cuts a short line across the bottom like an incision. The collar of my T-shirt. "They called us in the middle of the night, 2 AM maybe." She looks up at me, then back at her sketch. Keeps drawing. "Yeah, it was probably 2 AM"

"No . . . I didn't know that."

"Yes, they called." She slashes quick lines on the paper, out from the collar, curved at the ends. My shoulders. "They said that you had a gun and that you had run off to do something. They weren't sure what. But they couldn't find you."

I'm still biting my lip. "Oh . . . " I make myself take a drink of coffee. Breathe.

"And your father couldn't sleep. He kept sitting up in bed, in the dark. Not saying anything. Just sitting up. But that was it for me. I only sat up once."

She's drawing wildly now. Wrinkles in the T-shirt. Lines down and across. Shading. I'm watching her draw. I don't say anything.

"I sat up once in bed, just once, and I thought to myself, 'The Lord giveth, and the Lord taketh away.' I don't know why I thought that. 'The Lord giveth, and the Lord taketh away. Blessed be the name of the Lord.' And I went back to sleep. Right then. Just like that."

I put my hand on her right hand. The hand that isn't drawing. And her left hand, her drawing hand, slows down. It draws one line carefully, evenly, straight across the page, the edge of the table, as if an error, a mistake that cannot be reconciled.

I have my hand on her other hand, on top of that table.

⬛

CHAPTER 32

A Mentor

My father and I have spoken only once in the last six months. I've met my mother for coffee a few times during the spring, but never my father. When he calls and invites me over, I almost say I'm too busy, make an excuse. I don't know what we'll talk about. But I say, "Okay."

It is July. We sit in the wooden rockers on the front porch. I ease my chair into motion.

My father rocks too. He and Cooper have just returned from a medical mission trip to the Dominican Republic. Running health clinics in small villages. My father's forearms are tan.

"How have you been, Pete?"

I rock back and forth. "Good."

"Mmm. Good." My father eases his chair forward, stops, then eases it back, actions too slow for his personality. I know he's thinking. His eyes look tired.

Neither of us speak for a minute. I look out at the street. No cars.

"So, Pete, what have you been up to?"

"Not much. Reading, running, lifting weights. That's all I do every day." It's true. Mike goes out, but I don't. I don't leave the apartment except to run at night or score a new deal. And I'm barely doing that either. Just selling weed now, which I think of as an improvement.

I say, "It's the summer I do nothing."

My father doesn't ask how I pay my rent. He doesn't want to know.

I rock forward, stop my heels, then rock back. I think of fathers and sons, the books I've read in the past few months. "Hey, I read *Siddhartha*. And it was really good. About a father and a son. Do you want to read it?"

He stops his rocker. "Sure. Give me a copy." He wants us to be close. He'll work for it.

"Okay, I'll bring it over soon."

He taps his fingers on the arms of his chair. He's getting restless. "I know you earned that Fresh Start Scholarship to Lane. Are you still planning on going there?" He means the community college in the southeast hills. Mrs. Stahlberg set me up for the faculty-sponsored scholarship for troubled teens.

"Yeah, I think so. I'm gonna run cross-country for them, probably take English and writing classes."

"That's good," he taps his fingers more quickly. "But your mother and I have been talking. And if you want to . . . but only if you want to, you could apply to the U of O." He looks at me for my reaction.

I don't react at all. I just rock. Think about it.

Then he continues, "Even with the three expulsions on your record, you still have pretty good grades and SATs . . . and National Merit from the PSAT. You're smart . . . and you've got sports. Anyway, I think you'd get in, and we could help you. We would help pay."

"Hmmm." I rock. I realize that my father doesn't stress me out anymore. All that is over now. It's finished. And that surprises me. His offer to help pay for college feels like an offer, a possibility, a show of kindness. Only what it is.

My father stops rocking. "But just if you want to, I . . . " His fingers are tapping on the arms of the chair.

I smile. "I appreciate the offer, Dad. I do. And I'll think about it."

"Good, okay . . . Like I said, do what you want to do." His voice is calm, but his body is restless. He jumps up. "I've got to do some yard work today. But stay here. At the house. Stay here." He puts his hand out flat. "Coop and Hillary's boyfriend, Jay, are coming over in a little while. They'd love to see you. We'll smoke some cigars that I brought back from the DR. We had a great trip."

"Okay, Dad. I'll stay. That'd be good to see them."

My father steps back and stretches one of his calves on the front step. "Good," he says, then switches to the other leg.

Two nights earlier Cooper came over to my apartment with a fifth of Dominican rum and cigars he'd brought back from the island. Mike and I had a couple friends over, and we drank until we all started wrestling on the floor, then lay down and laughed for a long time, staring at the ceiling. We lit up Coop's cigars and told stories.

But Cooper isn't supposed to hang out with me, so I pretend as if that night didn't happen. "Yeah, I'd like to see Coop. It's been a long time."

That night, we sit out on my parents' porch and smoke cigars. Like men. My future brother-in-law Jay, Cooper, my father, and me. My father doesn't care that Cooper isn't old enough to smoke cigars. We're beyond that now. We're beyond a lot of things.

This is the first time that the voice makes sense to me. I am fifteen, a sophomore in high school. Late fall. My father and I are on a morning training run two weeks before the state cross-country meet. I am putting in extra mileage. My father has come along to get in an extra lecture.

This lecture is focused on the subject of dating too early, of breaking the family rules. My father usually reserves this lecture for the evening, every evening for the past three years, but Hillary has told him about my girlfriend at school, and that has earned me an extra morning lecture.

The lectures bore me. The lectures make me angry too, but I don't know that yet. I don't know that the anger is building. I think that I only feel boredom. I pick up the pace of our run to make it difficult for my father to talk to me.

I don't want to be bored.

My father begins breathing hard, and he says something that ends with " . . . deliberately disobeyed me."

I don't hear the rest. But it doesn't matter. I can recite this lecture from memory. It is always the same.

I feel the rhythm of my own breathing until the rhythm speeds up and flatlines, drones into a hum. I feel the hum coming like ripples circling out on a pond of blood. Then the hum is here. And the voice is here too, but in the background. Waiting. The voice always preceded by the buzz of the telegraph wires. I listen to the electricity in my head and wait for the voice, the monotone, the monotone I hear each day. I wait for the voice to give me simple instructions. I wait to be told. To obey. Sometimes I can anticipate the instructions, knowing the voice's intent before it speaks. When this happens, it feels good. It feels as though my brain is being washed over with warm water, rolling waves over my eyes.

I tap the ends of my fingers with my thumbs. I tap my fingers, listening and waiting. Counting. We are only two blocks from home. I count my steps and slow instinctively like a horse coming back in. I slow and listen for the voice.

And the voice begins. It begins in the middle of a sentence, as it has never begun before. I nod with it, nod and listen to its clear instructions. The voice is measured, patterned and smooth. Controlling. I listen to its rhythm and wait to obey.

Then I glance to my right and see my father's mouth. I see my father's mouth shaping the voice. His mouth producing the words. Even, smooth, monotonous, the words inside my head. My father is talking, and there is the voice, and the voice is with my father, and the voice is my father. His mouth creating the sentences inside my head, prescribing my life.

I never had an older brother, but my mother finds me one at church. His name is Tommy Glenn. He is a graduating senior at the University of Oregon, a fifth-year wrestler. When my mother meets him she says, "My name's Pam Hoffmeister. Do you want to be my son's mentor?" Only my mother is crazy enough to open a conversation with those two sentences.

Tommy says, "Huh?"

But my mother, undaunted, holds a piece of paper out to him. "Here's my son's pager number. He needs an older brother."

When Tommy pages me I have no idea who he is.

I call him back from the payphone at the Korean market. "Who is this?"

Tommy laughs. "Your mom wanted me to call and invite you to wrestle."

"What?"

Tommy laughs again. "Your mom, Pam Hoffmeister, she wants me to wrestle with you."

"Wrestle?"

"Yeah, I wrestled for the U of O. I just graduated. And she said you're a wrestler."

I tap the glass in the phone booth. "Uh, yeah. Kind of."

"So I'll pick you up in an hour? We'll go down to the Cas Center?"

"An hour?" I'm not doing anything. And for some reason I don't pretend to be busy. He can probably hear the shrug in my voice. I say, "Alright."

"Alright then. I'll pick you up in an hour, man."

Tommy walks like a Neanderthal, his fists swinging like clubs. He has no neck, just a head that angles down to big shoulders and biceps. He smiles most of the time.

I wear Tommy's U of O wrestling gear, shorts and a shirt and shoes that are two sizes too big.

Tommy crouches and says, "Shoot on me."

I shoot. Tommy knocks me to the ground with a shuck. When I get up, he's smiling.

He says, "No, really, man. Shoot on me."

I shoot a second time, faster, but he still knocks me to the ground. This time he has to bring his legs back a little, a sprawl to knock me down. I land on my face though. Hard. Tommy is still smiling when I get up.

Tommy crouches again. He says, "When you shoot, keep your head up. And even in practice, shoot as hard as you can."

I shoot again while he's still talking. I don't get his legs but I don't land on my face either. I get up. Shoot again. Then again. Then again.

After wrestling for an hour, we lift weights.

Tommy drives me home.

At my apartment Tommy says, "I'll pick you up tomorrow at four."

I nod. "Okay. Thanks." It's better than lifting weights by myself in my apartment.

Tommy flicks his thumb up. "No problem." Then he drives off.

Tommy shows up the next day right at four. And the next. We wrestle and lift weights every day.

After a couple of weeks Tommy calls me on a Saturday afternoon. He says, "What are you doing right now?"

"Reading. Why?"

"Well, I'm almost finished working now, and I was going to go to a movie with this girl, but she just got called in to work overtime. Anyway, I still want to see it. You wanna go?"

I look at my book cover. Put the book down. "Yeah, okay."

"Alright. Come down to Taylor's on Thirteenth. I get off in an hour."

I walk into Taylor's Bar forty-five minutes later. There's no bouncer at two in the afternoon. I sit down at the bar.

Tommy is dusting with a wet rag. "Want a beer, Pete?"

"Sure."

Tommy points to the taps. "Red Hook?"

"Yeah, thanks."

Tommy slides the pint into my hand. I take a sip. It's the first good beer I've ever had. Rich and bitter, nothing like the cheep beer we always steal from 7-Eleven.

I drink my pint as Tommy finishes his work. We leave when the new bartender shows up.

In the car, Tommy says, "So you're still dealing drugs, huh?"

"A little. I mean, not really. Barely."

Tommy says, "That's fucked up, man."

"Huh? No, I meant a *little*." I look at Tommy. He drives with one hand on top of the wheel.

He says, "I used to deal drugs too . . . with my older brother."

"You did?"

"Yep. My brother . . ." Tommy shakes his head and flexes his hand. It goes white.

I watch his face. "So you think dealing's wrong even if I only deal a little weed?"

Tommy looks over at me and laughs. "I don't *think* it's wrong. I *know* it's wrong."

"Really?"

"Yeah, really. Ask yourself this: Are you dealing this drug to kids?"

"Kids?"

"Are you dealing weed to anyone younger than you?"

Freshmen and sophomores are my whole business. They come to my apartment twice a week.

I don't say anything, and Tommy continues to drive.

| CHAPTER 33 |

⚏

The End of Boys

Tommy talks to the wrestling coach at the university. The university accepts rolling applications in the summer, but the coach makes sure my application is expedited. I'm accepted, and I take my father's offer for financial aid.

I move into a quad, one private room with a common bathroom and kitchen. I start painting pictures on my walls. Borrowing some of my mother's old acrylics, I sit up reading until midnight, then paint. I paint symbols and people and landscapes and still lifes. The walls begin to fill up like an old cave mapped in pictographs.

I start wrestling preseason, three-a-days with the University of Oregon. I am offered an official chance to walk on. I'll have to survive the first month and earn a spot on the team. I work hard. I am so tired each evening that I fall asleep before eating. I fall asleep, wake up, make dinner, read, and then paint.

My father gives me an old computer, and I start writing. I write until three in the morning. Write dreams. Write fiction. Try to write about my schools and my expulsions and traveling and Dallas. But I can't do it.

I never write about my family. How could I write about love and anger and truth and pain and compulsion and starting over?

I sit in my room alone at night, the one-hundred-watt ceiling bulb burning until three in the morning. I write bad fiction. Violent fiction. Semiautobiographical garbage.

Coop is out there. He is driving some girl's car. He calls me after midnight. "You awake, Pete?"

"Yeah."

"I'm going out to a party in Creswell. I was thinking about you. How have you been?"

"Good. Been wrestling a lot, and writing."

"That's good, man. That's dope. Hey, wanna come to this party with me?"

I am sitting at my little computer desk in the corner. I consider turning the computer off. Then I decide not to. "No, thanks, man. I think I'm gonna chill here tonight. Keep writing."

"Cool, cool. Well alright. I'm gonna go then. I love you, Pete."

"Love you too, Coop."

Coop and I hang out a few times that year. He drops by my apartment and sits on the floor. Looks at my paintings. We tell each other stories. Sometimes I go to his parties with him.

I watch him one night at a party. Watch him when he doesn't know I'm watching. He's sitting on a porch step with a joint in one hand and an Olde English forty in the other. High school kids are huddled around him. Kids older and younger. They aren't there for autographs or stickers or pictures yet. He's only a sophomore now and that will be years later. I will be mistaken for Coop then, at parties, at bars, out to eat. "You're Coop Hoffmeister, right? The pro snowboarder?"

I shake my head. "No, he's my brother."

"Oh," they try to hide their disappointment. Act polite. They say, "That's cool though. It's cool he's your brother, man."

We stand awkwardly, me and Coop's fan. Then I say, "Yeah, I get that a lot. It's fine. No problem."

"You know you look like him, huh? He's a sick rider, huh? Sick."

"Yeah, that's true," I agree. "He's a sick rider."

I take a creative writing course from Dorianne Laux, the poet. I don't know who she is, I just sign up for the course because I like to read and write. There are eleven students in the room, work-shopping poems around an oval table while Dorianne laughs and shakes her head. Her hair is always messy and she takes frequent smoke breaks, but her smile is wonderful.

All my poems are about my father or Cooper. I can't get away from them. I think Cooper is partying and fighting because of me, and I feel guilty.

I love and hate my father.

My poems are bad, with random line breaks and repetitive images. One line that recurs is "I hand Cooper a bloody axe." It would be better if that line was literal, but I'm afraid to write what's real.

Dorianne and I talk outside Columbia Hall. She says, "Well, what do you want to do?"

I hesitate. I've been in the course for two months now, and by this time I realize what an incredible writer she is. Her books and NEA awards are things we students talk about after class.

I say, "I think I want to write. I mean, I really like to write."

I've just gotten married, at age twenty, to a girl I dated for seven weeks, a beautiful, troubled girl named Jennie, someone who understands where I've been. My family supported the wedding. They invited the extended family, and my mother loaned Jennie her own wedding dress.

Ironically, Dorianne got married to her new husband, Joe, on the exact same day I did. We both laughed when we discovered this fact.

"Okay," Dorianne is smoking. She twists her mouth and blows smoke away from me. "Well then, why don't you write?"

I hook my thumbs in my backpack straps. Consider what she's saying. "Do you think I could? My poems aren't very good."

She doesn't agree or disagree. She takes a drag on her cigarette, waits, and exhales again sideways. "I think you have talent. At least story-wise . . . and imagistically."

I try not to smile but can't stop myself. I look away. Watch students come out of the Erb Memorial Union. "See, I want to write, but wrestling takes a lot of time. I don't know if I could write and wrestle at the same time. Or not well. Not both."

Dorianne shrugs. "So quit wrestling."

I laugh. "No, I don't think you understand. I've played a sport every season of every year since I was four years old."

She looks at me. She's read all my narrative poems. "Is this about you or your father?"

I don't know how to answer her. I think about that question a lot over the next few days. Then I quit the wrestling team and drop out of school.

The next spring, my wife, Jennie, and I volunteer with my father for a Medical Mission International trip to aid the Quechua Indians in the mountains of Ecuador. My father runs a general clinic in a church while Jennie works in the pharmacy. I teach health education, how to lift wood without tearing a hernia, how to boil water with a drop of Clorox to remove parasites.

One afternoon, my father and I hike up to a ridge at twelve thousand feet. The ridge sits on one flank of the volcano Imbabura, overlooking the town of Otavalo. We stand and admire the view.

My father says, "So what's your plan, Pete?" He means with school and life.

"I don't know. I've been thinking . . . Probably start school again in the fall. Go back."

He lifts his rebuilt shoulder and puts his arm around me. I'm bigger than him now, and he has to reach.

We look out at the town below us.

He says, "You know I don't care anymore, right?"

"Yeah."

"I don't care, Pete. I don't care what you do. I just want you to be happy."

I don't say anything.

He adds, "Whatever you decide is okay with me."

I can see our hotel down below us, two thousand feet down, a square Spanish stucco building.

"I'm thinking about a lot of things, Dad. Probably writing though. I like to write."

My father still has his arm around me. "Well, Pete, I've heard you talk about a lot of options: pediatric medicine, English, writing . . . history. And, like I said, I don't care what you decide. I just want you to do what *you* want to do."

I put my arm around him too now, and we stand looking out. Side by side. Arm over arm.

"I love you, Pete." I know he's tearing up because he always does.

"I love you too."

We don't say anything else. We stand there on top of that ridge and stare out at the colonial town below us. In the center, there are white Spanish buildings with red tile roofs. Around the outside, the stone houses of the Indians. Cars glint from far away, shiny flashes between buildings.

I reenroll in the fall and apply for the English Honors Program. They allow me to do a creative writing thesis with Dorianne, and we spend a year together working on a manuscript. She marks up my pages and smears chocolate chips in the margins. The story's no good, but I learn a lot about craft. How to write imagery. Consider word choice.

My English classes are small and I do well. I graduate with honors.

I work at a private school for a year and serve drinks at a restaurant. Then I go back to school again.

While I'm finishing my master's practicum, at twenty-three, I am asked to teach a quarter term of sixth-grade English and math. The class is normal for middle school: Awkward. Everyone in the room trying desperately to be cool. Heavy girls in low-cut tops. Four-foot boys with all the right pro-basketball gear.

I don't tell the students any stories about my life. I don't tell them anything. I teach English and math straight out of a book. I am a terrible teacher. I am even more bored than the students.

One afternoon, a small boy named Shane raises his hand.

I call on him.

"So, Mr. Hoffmeister, your brother is a pro snowboarder, right?"

"Yes. He is."

"And you're a teacher, right?"

"Yes, Shane." I smile. "I am."

The boy hesitates. I can tell that he wants to say something else. So I encourage him as a teacher should. "Go ahead, Shane. There are no dumb questions."

"Well," he cocks his head sideways, "what happened to *you?*"

I laugh. "Good question, Shane." Good question.

Cooper once asked the same question. I had finished my creative writing thesis in the English Honors Program at the university. Cooper had already given up a college football scholarship to be a sponsored snowboarder. He was beginning to travel and pick up magazine incentives.

We were home for dinner at my parents' house. Cooper was moving from Crested Butte, Colorado, to Mount Hood for the summer, and he was passing through Eugene. We were upstairs next to the stair railing where Cooper once punched me in the kidneys to pay me back for throwing him off the deck onto the concrete. We were next to that stair railing, and Coop's tone was like a kidney punch from behind. He said, "What happened to *you*, man?"

I was confused. "What do you mean?"

"What do *I* mean? I mean that *you've* changed."

I still didn't understand. "Yeah?"

"Yeah." He stepped toward me.

I thought about what he said. I said, "That's true, Coop. Maybe I have changed."

"*Maybe?*" he sneered. "No, man, you *have*. You've changed. And you know what?"

He was pissing me off now, so I said "*What*" as if I were throwing a counterpunch.

He nodded his head and smiled. "The truth is, *I* haven't changed. I'm exactly the same as I was in *eighth grade*."

I looked at him. All of him. I saw the scar on his forearm.

I saw the scar on my own forearm. The scar was from a party five years earlier. I was in Tennessee and thinking of Cooper and I took a cigarette from a girl and put it against the skin on my arm. Then I bent down and puffed on the cigarette. I burned a line up my arm slowly, carefully, a straight line two inches long.

The girl said, "What the *fuck* are you doing?" She didn't know me.

I said, "Nothing," and walked away still puffing on the cigarette that lay on my arm.

I put a check at the end of the burn, half an arrowhead etched into the flesh, the skin removed, a pink, separated gap, open like a fissure. Then I threw the rest of the cigarette into the bushes.

I called Coop later that night. I'd been drinking malt liquor, Mickey's and Olde English, like him.

I said, "Coop, I was thinking of you tonight, man. I burned half an arrowhead in my arm with a cigarette. You should burn the other half on your arm."

"Which way?" he asked.

I didn't know what he was talking about.

"Which way does your arrowhead go?" That was all Coop said.

"Oh," I said, "to the right."

"Okay. I got it." His voice was clear. "I'll burn mine to the left then."

I took a swig of my malt liquor and exhaled into the phone. "Good."

Coop agreed. "Good."

Coop's cigarette burn scarred nicely. It bubbled and thickened like a pink worm on his forearm.

My arrow faded. My skin wouldn't scar as I wanted it to. Everything went away. So we reburned my arm. We reburned it twice.

The second time, Coop and I were in the basement of our parents' house. It was dark down there by the workbench and the flickering of the lighter cast shadows on the workbench, the tools, the ceiling. The extralarge paperclip turned red in the flame. Coop held the paperclip steady with a pair of my father's pliers.

"Ready, Pete?"

I mumbled, "Yeah."

I wasn't drunk. I wasn't high. I was clear and purposeful and loved my brother more than anything. Burning my arm felt like eating my love.

I could hear Cooper's breath stop as he concentrated on gripping the paperclip with the pliers. I could feel the red paperclip break through my skin like boiling water through newspaper. I could smell the singed hair and the flesh opening.

I was a boy then. We were both just boys.

Afterword

I drop my younger daughter off at my parents' house to spend the night. My father is still at the hospital, and my mother is the only one home. They're going to make homemade pizza, watch a movie, create a princess fort out of my parents' bed.

My older daughter wishes she could stay too. She loves to paint with my mother and talk to her about books. Both girls know that my father will come home and take them out to buy candy or ice cream. He emails pictures of my girls smiling over desserts the size of their heads.

Fifteen years later, it's difficult to go forward and publish a book about one of the worst times in my family history. My parents and siblings would rather not look back. As Cooper says, "Back then, we were all fucking crazy."

And things are not perfect now. There is no total transformation, but a slow softening. To quote my mother, "We just have a big, messy family."

A year after dropping out of college, I reenrolled at the University of Oregon and finished my bachelor's degree. I began to write daily and publish sporadically with lit journals and magazines. But mostly, my writing was rejected.

I taught for a year at a private school. I wanted to share good books and the process of writing. I wanted to impact young people with my story, to teach them that failure is not the end.

I started rock climbing, and the pursuit became my number one pastime, a practice of fear and meditation, balance and precision. I love the gymnastic movements and chess-like details.

I go hiking and climbing with my wife, Jennie. Cook with her. Camp with her. Talk and trade good books. Watch storms. Play Trivial Pursuit.

I hang out with my brothers and sisters too. Laugh and tell stories. Have a new understanding of Jesus's Beatitudes.

I get up in the dark and write at the dining room table until light sifts through the kitchen window and my older daughter taps me on the shoulder: Time to go sit on the couch and read *Calvin and Hobbes*.

My obsessive-compulsive issues have been minimized. I might feel like buttoning and unbuttoning the third button on my dress shirt thirty-three times during thirteen minutes, but I can stop myself. Will myself to relax.

When I check to see if my alarm clock is set for the thirteenth time each night, Jennie just says, "Stop," and smiles at me.

Two years after finishing my English degree, I completed the Master's of Arts in Teaching program at Pacific University and applied for an opening at my alma mater, South Eugene High School. In my interview for South, I said that my three high school expulsions would help me to understand struggling students. And during my career there, the school counselors and administrators have regularly placed disillusioned, addicted, abused, and paroled students in my classes.

While I love my students in general, I feel a great responsibility toward troubled young people.

In 2005 my good friend and colleague Jeff Hess and I started the Integrated Outdoor Program, combining environmental literature with outdoor pursuits such as hiking, kayaking, rafting, snow camping, map and compass work, spelunking, rock climbing, and survival. We want our students to feel a deeper connection to the natural world and recognize the disconnect that technology and online socializing bring. We hope for the simple lessons of nature, the interaction of weather and decision-making, adventure and clear consequences.

Cooper tore his posterior cruciate ligament returning a kickoff his senior year in high school and lost all chances of playing Division I college football, his lifelong dream. But he took a Division II scholarship to Western State University in Colorado and discovered that snowboarding in the backcountry near Gunnison, Colorado, was an even greater draw than jumping a slant route or staying home for a crack on a wide receiver's reverse. Cooper earned his first snowboarding sponsorship from a local board shop that freshman year in college, then dropped out of school to pursue riding full-time. He's been a professional snowboarder for more than ten years, riding for Never Summer, Skullcandy, and NEFF.

As rock climbing does for me, snowboarding gives Cooper the adventure and danger he needs, the passion and explosion. He's made a career of throwing himself off of sixty-foot cliffs and over one-hundred-foot gaps. The ice tempers him. The mountains are his soul.

■

In 2005 Cooper asked me to get an online divinity degree so that I could legally marry him to his longtime girlfriend, Carrie. We held the ceremony in the same backyard where I was married eight years earlier.

Cooper is still the most loyal person I know.

Hillary and I don't sit on the carpet and play Speed for hours, but we will stay up late talking past dark when she's in town. She and her husband, Jay, both encouraged me as I wrote this book and supported me during the publication process. Even though Hillary knew the subject matter would be difficult, that she wouldn't always look good as a teenage sister in the book, she called different family members and repeated the question, "Are we going to support Peter's art or not?"

My younger sister Haley calls me one night. She has a role in a movie. She tells me about that. Then she recounts a funny story about my nephew being afraid of a bunk bed, and she imitates his voice. We talk for more than an hour.

Often lost in the family chaos, Haley survived and went on to study comedy with the Groundlings in Los Angeles. Although she was the toughest female Smashball player of all time, I always admired her kindness and sense of humor.

Ellis and Maddie were raised by my parents, but in a different family. In their childhoods, my parents allowed television, sleeping in on the weekends, and quitting sports midseason. Two years ago, Ellis was one of my favorite students in the Integrated

Outdoor Program. He's now in college, studying dance and premed. Maddie, the youngest, is majoring in fine arts.

My father still works as a neonatologist. He is often asked about retirement but loves working with premature newborns and will probably continue to work until his late seventies. On his days off, he plays golf or takes his grandchildren bowling. During furloughs from work, he leads medical teams to Haiti, the Dominican Republic, and Guatemala.

As often as we can, we try to catch a baseball game together.

My mother paints with oils every day, working on a long series of paintings called "The Undocumented," impressionist and fauvist work honoring illegal immigrants in the United States.

She loves the desert, the sky, Kathleen Norris, and the Catholic Church.

On hearing that this book was going to print, she wrote a letter to me that said I was her "hero as a persevering artist." Since she taught me the inherent value of art, walked through countless painting exhibits, and explained the habits of long-dead sculptors, all while wearing clothes stained by gesso and Cray-Pas, I'd have to turn that sentence back on her.

I used to admire Barry Lopez's line from *Desert Notes*, when his character says he wants to trick blood from a rock and cut the devil in half. But I don't want to trick anything anymore. I just want to live the daily life, eat meals with Jennie and the girls, camp on BLM land, climb rocks, swim rivers, and fish.

Mostly, I want to hold my two daughters each morning, my two greatest stories.

| ACKNOWLEDGMENTS |

First, always, thank you, Jennie. When I looked at you in that dirty motel room thirteen years ago and said, "We'll never have any money because I want to be a writer," you said, "I never liked money anyway." Thank you for that, and for so many other things that I could never mention them all. Your belief was incredible. This book would not have happened without you.

To my mother, who always made art seem like the highest calling of the church. A sacred life. A devotion. For all the words and books and writers and painters and discussion and wonder. And for the smell of oil and turpentine in my childhood. Thank you.

To my father, who taught me the value of early mornings and hard work. You said, "Well, Pete, sometimes early morning is the only time to get things done." I believed you and respected your consistency. This book was born in the morning. Also, for your love of traveling and adventure, languages and people in need. Thank you.

To Jose Chaves, who tossed aside my crappy first novel attempt and said, "Don't write this. Your memoir is the book you have to write." Jose, may there be dark coffee in heaven for you.

To Cooper, of course. We lived it, and blood is blood.

To Haley, for a younger sister's belief; to Hillary, for putting up with me during my sophomore year; to Ellis, for coffee dates; and to Maddie, for the peaceful moments holding you while watching World Series games. You were beautiful.

I still say "Hoffmeisters don't quit."

To the three women who were kind to me when I needed it most, Pris Wilt, Bonnita Stahlberg, and Dorianne Laux. To Ben Dodge for the Bring Pete Hoffmeister Home Fund. And to Yeoman for the $60.

To Aimee, for sitting on the back porch with me; to Courtney, for our games of pool; and to Betsie, for that one important phone call from the road in Central Oregon.

To Garth, Sarah, and Nate, for listening to the first three chapters out loud at the cabin even though you, Nate, had to walk it off in the kitchen.

Thank you, Jay, for the picture that doesn't exist of you and Annabelle at the Dallas book signing. The morning after our dinner together.

To Aunt Dan and the boys, for fishing. And for whispering into the phone, "Help me, Peter. Help me."

Thank you to Caleb for the video and for setting aside so many hours during one of the busiest times in your life.

To Literary Arts for validation, for the encouragement and financial support of me as an emerging writer in the state of Oregon. To Susan Denning. And to Miriam Gershow, my fellowship cowinner, for your willingness to read my words.

To Adriann Ranta, my wolf at Wolf, the first person in the book world to say "I am completely in love with it." I think you always knew I'd come back to you.

Thank you to Siri Comeau for honest, clear revision advice on draft number twelve. I don't know why you read it, but I am grateful. Thirteen is now lucky.

To Kirsten Wolf for helping with the low point. Plus reading on short notice.

To Ben LeRoy for support and humor. What artist can survive without either of those?

Thank you to my editor, Denise Oswald, for an hour-long conversation on a borrowed cell phone out of Camp 4 Yosemite.

And for all the excellent revision and edit notes. I was blessed to have you.

Thank you to Jack Shoemaker for taking on an ugly orphan.

And to so many others at Soft Skull and Counterpoint: Laura Mazer, Charlie Winton, Sarah Cantor, and Maren Fox.

Also to my copyeditor, Mikayla Butchart, for that one word.

To the readers and friends who didn't laugh in my face when I said that I wanted to write books: Queen Eileen, Ingy, A-Dre, JHess, River, Zach, Bri-Bri, Bobbie, Corrina, Kathie, Evelyn Hess, Ellie, Tim, Sarah Palin, Lee, Amy, Dane, Garrick, Shannon, and Mike Wilt, my Camp Sherman brother.

To my students who have become friends: Sonja Jameson, Whitney Cox, and Mike Holmes.

And finally, to my daughters, who learned to ask way too young, "Is your book going to be published?"

I say, "Yes."